IMAGES
of Sport

ACCRINGTON STANLEY FOOTBALL CLUB

In training for the last big FA Cup tie ever played by Accrington Stanley as a League club are, from left to right: George Hudson, Jackie Swindells, Mike Ferguson, Jimmy Harrower. Stanley had been paired with First Division Preston North End in the third round of the 1960/61 FA Cup. Superbly marshalled by player-manager Harrower, Stanley secured a highly creditable 1-1 draw in the first tie at Deepdale before going down in the replay in front of nearly 15,000 fans at Peel Park.

IMAGES
of Sport

ACCRINGTON STANLEY FOOTBALL CLUB

Compiled by
Phil Whalley

TEMPUS

Tempus Publishing Limited
The Mill, Brimscombe Port,
Stroud, Gloucestershire, GL5 2QG

ISBN 0 7524 2248 0

Typesetting and origination by
Tempus Publishing Limited
Printed in Great Britain by
Midway Colour Print, Wiltshire

Dedication

To the memory of my grandfather, Jack Cronshaw, my first Crown Ground chaperone.

Stanley captain Dave Hargreaves is presented with the Cheshire League Second Division championship trophy, on 22 May 1981.

Contents

Acknowledgements

This book could not have been put together without the help of many people, and I would like to thank them for the time, energy and trust that they placed at my disposal. I have had the pleasure of talking to some of Stanley's ex-players in both League and non-League, and all provided valuable information and photographs. Thanks to Don Bramley, Joe Devlin, Chris Grimshaw, Alex Hamilton, Dave Hargreaves, David Hinksman, Jimmy Hinksman, Bill McInnes, Jimmy Mulkerrin, Dave Thornley, Keith Walkden and Ian Wilcox. I also received the very kind help of Mrs Joan Croasdale, who arranged the photograph of her father Jack Wigglesworth's FA long service medal, and who also provided me with other photographs and helped with the identification of players.

Those involved at the Crown Ground today have also been very helpful and accommodating. Thanks to John DeMaine, Phil Terry, Terry Slinger and Eric Whalley for their help with this project. Other Accrington Stanley enthusiasts and collectors have been of great assistance in providing prints, advice and information. Thanks are due to John Alty, Eric and Joan Butterfield, Garth Dykes, Mary Gregory, Jean Harrison, Mike Jackman, Robert Jones, Jack and Mildred Knowles, Ray Simpson and Brent Whittam. I must especially thank Alan Clegg, who showed the most extraordinary trust in letting me borrow freely from his eye-opening collection of Accrington Stanley memorabilia.

Clearly with any book of this kind, the co-operation of local newspapers and photographers is absolutely vital, and I would like to thank Chris Lloyd and Howard Talbot for their kind co-operation. Jim Wilkinson of the *Accrington Observer* was most obliging, allowing me to borrow from their archive. The role of the *Accrington Observer* in both chronicling and assisting Accrington Stanley through the years is inestimable and a model example of how important a local newspaper can be to a football club. Thanks also to John Napier and Charmaine Wright of the *Lancashire Evening Telegraph*, whose photographs were particularly helpful for the final two chapters. The Local Studies section of Accrington Library was also most helpful; my thanks to everyone there, especially Helen Barrett, who patiently dealt with many requests and offered numerous suggestions. Thanks are also due to James Howarth and Liz Mabley at Tempus Publishing for their advice and enthusiasm.

Lucky is the writer who can count on supportive family and friends, and I would like to thank some special people who have encouraged me all the way: Karen Neill provided much appreciated, unconditional support, even when it meant precious annual leave spent in the library. Gill Hartley and Steve and Veronica Cross were always ready with their unique and wonderful hospitality. Gerard Grimshaw provided some valuable contacts, as did David Whalley, with whom I am in additional debt due to the great deal of time he spent helping me with photographs and players. My parents, Roy and Chris Whalley, also provided some valuable contacts. Love and thanks to all.

Saving my greatest debt to last, this book would have been impossible to produce without the assistance of Garth Dawson. Garth has chronicled in celluloid the fortunes of his home town team for many years, and a good deal of the photographs that appear in the following pages are his work, many of which he reproduced specially for this book. It was more help than I had the right to expect, and my heartfelt thanks go to Garth for his time and generosity.

Phil Whalley
May 2001

Introduction

Football has been played in Accrington almost since the very origins of the organised game. The late 1860s saw local papers like the *Accrington Herald* take an interest in games played in the locality, providing the results of early fixtures, and occasionally small match reports. It is often observed that many of today's Football League clubs owe their genesis to enthusiasts within churches and cricket clubs, but occasionally the seed can be found within groups of tradesmen.

An early example of this is in Accrington, where the town's tailors used to arrange a football match each year. The *Accrington Times* of 19 November 1870 offers us a glimpse into these early days of football. The match took place on a Monday afternoon, which meant a very welcome half-day holiday. The ad-hoc nature of the arrangements can be seen in the instruction: 'All tailors in Accrington who wish to engage in the match must leave their names with the Secretary before twelve o'clock on the day of play'. It was probably the case that any team list was entirely arbitrary until it was established who was there. Nonetheless, all participants were promised a full dinner.

A more inclusive and established celebration was the Grand Gala of Sunday Schools, held each August in the town. In 1871, John Hargreaves' Barn Field was the venue. Hargreaves was an important local philanthropist who would become a central figure in organised Accrington football. In the town-wide celebration that was the Sunday School gala, the keenness of Accrington's young men for the association game was there for all to see: 'A number of boys and young men found football to be a lively and entertaining exercise. Once or twice it was kicked around the field and created a little consternation when it happened to fly among a group of young ladies.'

Such games as the tailors' match and the kickabout at the Sunday School gala are seen as the precursors to more formalised team football, and were common throughout the north of England at this time. Trends elsewhere in Accrington indicated a fast-developing locality: many public buildings, schools and churches were built in this period, including the Market Hall (opened in 1869) and the Police Station (1871). This rapid development clearly pointed to the growing status of the town, cemented in 1878 when it received its charter and became a municipal borough.

There is some evidence that an Accrington town football team played as early as 1876, this being the year that some members within Accrington Cricket Club first aired the idea of forming an association football team, as neighbours Church and Enfield already had. However, it is in 1878 that the tradition of organised Accrington football is truly founded, for July of this year saw a meeting of some of the town's dignitaries and football enthusiasts in Abbey Street's Black Horse pub, and the decision was made to form Accrington Football Club.

Letters to the press in the immediate aftermath of this decision were encouraging, and the club itself wasted little time. On 14 September 1878, an advertisement in the *Accrington Times* appealed for players to attend a practice match, and just two weeks later, on 28 September, Accrington Football Club played its first ever competitive game of association football, against Church Rovers.

Thus began the long association between Accrington and organised team football. This association was to see Accrington represented among some of the pioneers of the game and involved in some of the game's defining moments. Along with Church and Enfield, Accrington FC was a founder member of the Lancashire FA, formed in 1878. In 1884, no less than four Accrington teams (Accrington FC, Accrington Grasshoppers, Bell's Temperance and Peel Bank Rovers) were represented at the meeting which threatened to form a secessionist British Football Association. This manoeuvre successfully forced the legalisation of professional football in England, though not before Accrington FC had been temporarily expelled from the FA in 1883 for that very offence. And of course, perhaps most famously of all, Accrington FC was a founder member of the Football League itself, evidence, if any were needed, that the town had established its own identity in the face of larger neighbours.

That the 'Owd Reds' lasted only five seasons in the Football League underscores some themes that recur throughout the history of Accrington football. Money has nearly always been a problem for Accrington clubs. As early as 1886, Accrington FC were running a 6d lottery, with the prize for the lucky winner of a dwelling house worth £150, and in 1890 were among the first group of professional clubs to issue shares as a means of raising money. To their credit, the club set the price of its shares at ten shillings, significantly lower than most clubs, and appealed for ordinary townspeople to invest in their local club.

Their appeal failed, and the club succumbed to financial pressures just three years later. This brings us to the second, and not uncontroversial theme. As Accrington FC resigned from the Football League in 1893, unable to pay its debts, the Accrington public stood accused of not supporting their town team. It was the first such accusation, but its echo has sounded through almost every following decade to the present day. Whatever the merits of such accusations, I hope that in the tale that follows, all Accrington supporters and sympathisers may reflect upon the need of all local town teams for enthusiastic support, free from the damage inflicted by cynicism.

One

Origins and Early Struggles 1891-1916

	FIXTURES			
Date	Club	G.	F.	A
Sep. 1	Bell's Reserve	A		
,, 8	Knuzden	A		
,, 15	Oswaldtwistle Wand.	H		
,, 22	St. Augustine's	H		
,, 29	Baxenden	A		
Oct. 6	St. Augustine's	H		
,, 13	Oswaldtwistle Wand.	A		
,, 20				
,, 27	Baxenden	H		
Nov. 3	Knuzden	H		
,, 10				
,, 17	Huncoat	H		
,, 24				
Dec. 1	N.E.L.A.			
,, 8	Bell's Reserve	H		
,, 15	Huncoat	A		
,, 22				
,, 25				
,, 29				

	FIXTURES—continued			
Date	Club	G.	F.	A.
Jan. 1				
,, 5	N.E.L.A.			
,, 12				
,, 19				
,, 26				
Feb. 2	N.E.L.A.			
,, 9				
,, 16				
,, 23				
Mar. 2	N.E.L.A.			
,, 9				
,, 16				
,, 23				
,, 30				
Apr. 6	N.E.L.A.			
,, 13				
,, 20				
,, 27				

In March 1962, when the demise of Accrington Stanley was known throughout football, the *Accrington Observer* had the foresight to track down the lone surviving member of the group of players who formed the original Accrington Stanley. His name was Fred Carr, and he recalled that the suggestion to start the football team that became Accrington Stanley was made in 1891 by two patrons of the Stanley Arms, located on Stanley Street. This team was first known as Stanley Villa, and comprised of young lads from the Peel Park district of the town. Although Stanley Villa was never sufficiently senior to enter a competitive league, the team enjoyed enthusiastic support from the locals. It was the demise in 1893 of Accrington FC that inspired those behind Stanley Villa to adopt the name of their town. Accrington Stanley was born.

Stanley's first competitive season of football was their 1894/95 campaign in the Accrington and District League, and they produced the fixture card (above) for their supporters. The fixture against Knuzden on 3 November was the occasion of a late disallowed goal and a subsequent pitch invasion which rendered the game void. This caused something of a stir in the press, and the game was only replayed at the end of the season, by which time Stanley were vying for the title with Knuzden. A 1-2 defeat consigned Stanley to the runners-up spot, but this impressive start saw the club move up a grade the following season, competing in the North East Lancashire League.

Accrington Stanley were just one of a number of teams who adopted the town name: Grasshoppers, Wanderers, Villa, Amateurs, and Borough were among the others. The sudden resignation of Accrington FC from the Football League meant that these local amateur teams were now the most senior sides in the area. Here, then, truly was an opportunity for the most ambitious young footballers and administrators to pick up the baton dropped by Accrington FC and once more seek to advance the game in their home town. One man who picked up the standard with particular determination and marched with great distinction was John Haworth, nephew of Accrington FC's famous captain and England international, George 'Jud' Haworth.

John Haworth *(right)* played locally with Meadow Bank Rovers, but his ambition was far grander: to re-establish the professional game in Accrington. In 1894, at the age of just eighteen, Haworth took over the managership of Meadow Bank Rovers, and three years later he disbanded the club and brought his players to Accrington Stanley, where he became a committee member. Within months he was team manager, a position from which he could make strides towards his ambition.

Haworth's first full season as manager – 1897/98 – saw Stanley win the North East Lancashire League title, and this season also saw the club move from Moorhead Park to Woodnook. The latter had been the home of Bell's Temperance FC, a team good enough to twice win the Lancashire Junior Cup in the mid-1880s. By 1894, Bells had ceased to function and Stanley shared the Woodnook ground with Accrington Villa. The pitch sloped terribly, and the players had to change at the nearby Brittania Inn, on Nuttall Street. Despite the spartan surroundings of the Bells ground, the next few years saw the emergence of Accrington Stanley from relative amateur obscurity to become the senior non-League side in the area. An important element of this was the raising of the club's standing through a number of high-profile acquisitions, including ex-England international Jimmy Whitehead, who was signed from Blackburn Rovers.

Interest was further heightened in 1901 by the success of the club in gaining admittance to the Lancashire Combination. This was the most senior amateur competition in the area and was the league in which the reserve sides of most of the county's professional teams were entered. For an amateur team on the rise, the Lancashire Combination was the place to be, offering the chance to lock horns with the big Football League clubs like Everton, Blackburn Rovers, Manchester City, Liverpool and Preston North End. A successful first season in the Combination saw the Stanley committee gamble on a move back to the smarter surroundings of Moorhead Park for the start of the 1902/03 season. The Saturday half-day was instituted wholesale in Accrington's mills in January 1902, and the club probably hoped for increased gates as a consequence.

Accrington Stanley, 1902/03. From left to right, back row: W. Chadwick (committee member), J. Finney, Coupe, Boulton, S. Emmett (trainer). Middle row: H. Morgan, Golding, J. Bradshaw, W. Bradshaw, Gardner. Front row: A. Watkins, M. Brunton, J. Hargreaves. Stanley were now a semi-professional outfit, whose players expected payment and whose administration involved full-time employment. The financial pressures now surrounding the club had been reflected in March 1901 when the Lancashire FA suspended the club and its officials over the retention of £5 19s from the gate of a Lancashire Junior Cup tie. It is very likely that the club's management knew full well what was going on, and they may have even sanctioned the action. In order that the suspension be lifted, the club's treasurer fell on his sword in return for (rumour has it) a new overcoat.

It was fortunate for the club that this turned out to be the end of the matter, as the team assembled by the board and management continued to flourish. With a free-scoring striker in Matt Brunton, the Accrington Stanley team pictured above made a small piece of history in 1902/03 by becoming the first ever non-League team to win the Lancashire Combination, dethroning Manchester City Reserves in a thrilling finale to the season. The performances of Billy Bradshaw earned him a contract at Blackburn Rovers, and he went on to win international honours with England whilst at Ewood Park.

Even without the talent of Billy Bradshaw in the side, 1903/04 was another highly successful season for Stanley. Once again they challenged for the Lancashire Combination title, with Everton Reserves being their principal rivals, but this time it was the professional club that prevailed. Stanley regrouped for another campaign and the squad pictured above is that of 1905/06 which again captured the Lancashire Combination championship for Accrington. Stanley had thus won the Combination two times in four seasons. Manager John Haworth is pictured far right, whilst club stalwart Jack Bradshaw is in the centre of the middle row. With such achievements under his belt, Haworth was emerging as a real managerial talent.

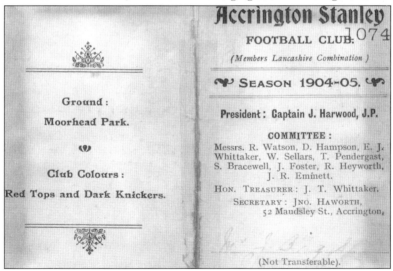

Lancashire Combination football in the early years of the twentieth century was an attractive proposition for the football enthusiasts of Accrington. With a number of prestigious professional clubs sending their second teams to Moorhead Park, Stanley met the demand for season tickets at an early stage. This example is from 1904, although the club may have issued season tickets before this.

Accrington Stanley with the Combination trophy, August 1906. As two-times champions of one of the strongest non-League competitions in the north of England, Accrington Stanley was established as the senior semi-professional club in the area. In 1907, the decision was taken to incorporate the club as a limited company, and £1,000 worth of shares was successfully issued. The president of the club, Captain John Harwood, bought thirty shares. Harwood was well known in the football community for his own annual award of a set of medals to the non-League team that finished highest in the Lancashire Combination, medals that his own team won in 1902 and 1904.

Stanley line-up during the 1906/07 season. As befitted a top non-League side, Accrington Stanley enjoyed a significant FA Cup run in 1907, including an elimination of Crewe Alexandra 1-0 at Moorhead Park after an initial 1-1 draw. In the second round proper, Stanley met First Division Bradford City, and took home a share of the 16,000 gate and most of the plaudits after a brave 0-1 defeat.

Stanley line up in their white away strip at a wintry venue during the 1907/08 season. From left to right, back row: T. Pendergast (chairman), Carter, Gaskell, Randall, Shaw, Whittaker. Front row: Stott, Wilson, Chadwick, Bradshaw, Brindle, McGuigan, Garside.

If the years up to 1907 were characterised by constant progress and achievement, the following few saw Stanley confronted with the problem of where to go from the position they had so valiantly earned for themselves. Other non-League clubs from bigger Northern conurbations, such as Stockport County and Oldham Athletic, had emulated Stanley's achievements in winning the Lancashire Combination, but both had subsequently secured full membership of the Football League. These clubs could, however, count on substantial crowds from far greater local populations than Accrington, at this point a town of just 45,000 people. As Oldham flourished and won promotion to the First Division, Stanley remained in the Lancashire Combination.

In the seasons of 1908/09 and 1909/10, the Moorhead Park faithful enjoyed two more good FA Cup runs. In 1908/09, Stanley fought their way through a preliminary round and four qualifying rounds before an unusual draw at home to the amateur Northern Nomads club. A few of the spectators present that November day might have remembered the expulsion of Accrington FC from the FA in 1883 for professionalism, a ruling made at the hands of the kind of determinedly amateur, ex-public school men that made up the Nomads team. No doubt a few choice Lancashire phrases greeted the Nomads, and the amateur gentlemen of the game caused the town's football supporters yet more grief, defeating Stanley 2-0.

The following season, at the expense of Haslingden and Brentford, Stanley advanced to the first round proper, where they hit the jackpot with an away tie at Blackburn Rovers. They were crushed 1-7 at the hands of what was then one of the best teams in the land, but a consolation was a share of the receipts from a large paying attendance. However, disaster struck just one month later, when a severe storm destroyed the main stand at Moorhead Park. The repair bill wiped out the profits from the FA Cup tie at Blackburn, and this was typical of the club's fortune at this time.

Stanley in action at Moorhead Park, 1910. At the end of the 1909/10 season, John Haworth, still only thirty-four but in his thirteenth season as manager of Accrington Stanley, successfully applied for the managership of Burnley. His welcome in the pages of the *Burnley Express* revealed something of the changes he had overseen at Moorhead Park, including a rise in the weekly wage bill from 30s to £30. The paper also noted that: 'In the Accrington district, he was respected as a man of tact and talent, for he can manage players with the velvet gloves and conceal a will of iron.' Clearly, Accrington Stanley's growth into a major non-League club was down in no small measure to the vision and ambition of their manager, who went on to win promotion, the FA Cup and the League Championship with Burnley.

That wage bill of £30 per week was by no means large by pre-war football standards, but 1911 saw a schism within the Lancashire Combination that had severe financial implications for clubs of Stanley's rank. In an attempt to wrest more power from the League clubs on the Combination executive, the non-Leaguers met in caucus to organise their actions. When the details of this meeting were revealed, the League clubs, led by Manchester United, resigned from the Lancashire Combination in protest and formed the Central League.

The loss of League clubs was a severe blow to the status of the Lancashire Combination, and the effects of this loss – especially of decreased attendances – was exacerbated by a rash of industrial unrest. Striking men had little money to spare, though the sixpence for the football was often the last non-essential to go. In August 1911, the railwaymen went out on strike, and the following month saw a strike at Riley's that led to seventeen arrests. Sure enough, the combination of falling gates and the financial demands of a semi-professional club dragged Accrington Stanley into serious debt. In 1912/13, Stanley again challenged for the Lancashire Combination title, but without the patronage of League clubs the competition was desperately lacking in authority or glamour. Stanley eventually finished runners-up to Eccles Borough, but were disastrously eliminated from the FA Cup in their first tie at Rochdale. By the start of the 1913/14 campaign, only the funds raised by a pre-season gala prevented the club from going into receivership.

The season of 1914/15 was the last official 'peacetime' season, though the moral appropriateness of competitive football was questioned by the outbreak of the First World War on the eve of the season. Stanley completed their last season of peacetime football in a respectable sixth position and competed in the 1915/16 season of wartime football, but the criminal sacrifice of the Accrington Pals at the Somme on 1 July 1916 understandably put paid to Accrington Stanley's activities for the duration. In 1916, the stands, dressing rooms and boundary hoardings of Moorhead Park were all sold and Accrington Stanley went into hibernation.

Two
Something from Nothing
1919-1939

A young Dick Webster (back row, far right) in what is thought to be an Accrington Stanley youth team, around 1936/37. Webster made his first team debut as an eighteen-year-old in January 1938 and was bought a year later by Sheffield United for £1,000. After the war, Webster returned to Peel Park, where he was a valued player until his retirement through injury in 1951.

A full Accrington Stanley line-up, August 1919. In May 1919, it was decided that the forthcoming September would see the commencement of competitive football, and the new season was eagerly awaited. Letters in the *Accrington Observer* as early as February 1919 expressed a desire to reawaken the town's football team. Accrington Stanley was still in existence, but was in debt and had no assets. The rental of Moorhead Park was now beyond Stanley's means, and so with the help of a dedicated group of fundraisers, the club raised the cash to buy Peel Park, a mere plot of land at that stage, but with the advantage of being relatively close to the town centre. Demonstrating a sense of goodwill that is essential to any small town club, the Education Committee of Accrington Council allowed the club to use the changing rooms of the adjacent school. With these foundations in place, Accrington Stanley once again represented the town in the Lancashire Combination in season 1919/20. This photograph shows the club and its many helpers before the commencement of the new season.

Such was the haste with which the club had had to reorganise, the pitch had no drainage system and was marked length-wise alongside the school, from Manor Street to the Peel Park Hotel. In terms of playing staff, Stanley relied mostly on local players. Stanley's first fully competitive match for four and a half years ended in a 0-7 defeat at Tranmere, in which George Chapman, the only Accrington player with any substantial Football League experience, missed a penalty.

Despite, or maybe because of, a swamp of a pitch, Stanley recovered from this dreadful start to finish the season in mid-table. The summer recess allowed the club to lay drains and reorientate the pitch down the slope to face the school, but this could not have been done without Stanley's remarkable band of helpers, pictured here in 1921 outside the Supporters' Club office. The club cannily decided to open their new ground 'officially', and organised a series of fundraising events in celebration.

Accrington Stanley v. Chorley, 18 September 1920. Chorley were the guests for the official opening, and the event was a huge success all round as 10,000 townsfolk turned up to see Stanley defeat the Magpies 2-0. Four days later, Blackburn and Burnley sent their reserve sides to Peel Park for another fundraiser. Perhaps as a favour for his old club, Burnley manager John Haworth included two first team players, one being star centre forward Joe Anderson, scorer of 31 League and Cup goals that season as part of Burnley's Championship-winning side. Not surprisingly, Anderson ran riot in the friendly, scoring seven goals in a 10-1 victory.

Accrington Stanley, with the Lancashire Junior Cup, 1920/21. From left to right, standing: J. Jacques, E. Chadwick, F. Hayes, G. Holman, R. Cragg, C. Smithies, G. Chapman, G. Wilson, J. Yates, J. Tattersall, H. Smethurst, A. Colwell, T. Heslop, J. Richardson, T. Pendergast, J. Sutcliffe, A. Stoddard, E. Hargreaves. Seated: J. Brown, J. Holland, J. Miller, C. Pearson, P. Nelis, P. Quigley, A. Stevenson, S. Pilkington (secretary), F. Brennand (trainer), J. Parramore. Front: unknown, W. Pilkington (mascot).

With football now a hugely popular game, the authorities took the step of extending the Football League, and during the 1920/21 season Stanley accepted an invitation to join the newly proposed Third Division. The club ended their days in the Lancashire Combination on a high note, defeating Chorley in the final of the Lancashire Junior Cup at Ewood Park in front of 20,000 spectators.

In March 1921, Accrington Stanley was elected to the Third Division (North) and the club set about organising their finances accordingly. After a series of meetings, the club decided to form itself into a limited liability company, whilst the ever-resourceful supporters came up with some winning ideas to raise funds. According to Stanley's first programme, published in January 1921, the supporters had that season raised half of a £2,000 target towards the building of terraces and a stand extension. In August 1921, the last formality of incorporation was completed, and Accrington Stanley FC (1921) Ltd prepared to carry the town's standard within the Football League once more. It had been thirty-three years since Accrington FC had embarked upon the same adventure, and little over thirty years since regulars at the Stanley Arms had suggested that Fred Carr and his mates organise a team.

Accrington Stanley's maiden season in the Football League was to see great hopes dashed by ill fortune. By mid-March 1922, an unblemished home record of thirteen straight wins saw Stanley challenging at the top of the division, helped by a settled defence and the presence of a free-scoring striker in Patrick Nelis. By the end of March, Stanley had lost both full-backs to crippling injuries, and had sold Nelis to Nottingham Forest for a £2,000 fee, considered too good to refuse. In effect, this was the end of Stanley's season too, with five defeats in their last seven games resulting in a final position of fifth. A clear-out concluded the season's cycle, and even at this nascent stage, the pattern familiar to many Stanley supporters can be discerned: pre-season hope eroded by financial worries, undone by misfortune, undermined by ill-considered transfers and finally extinguished by a spate of releases which confirmed that some of the players had not been good enough in the first place.

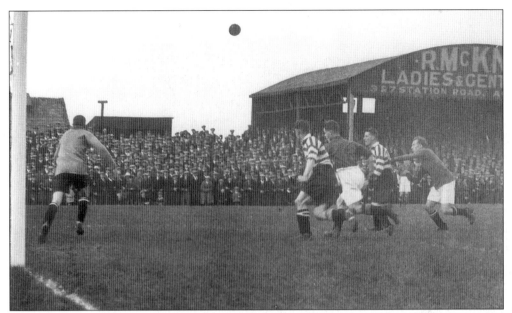

Thought to be an early season clash with Darlington around 1922/1923, this depicts an all-too-rare sight of a virtually full house at Peel Park. Frustratingly, gates tended to decline dramatically after the early season fixtures. Unfortunately, this was also a period of struggle for many of Accrington's workers. In March 1922, the AEU union took 5,000 workers out on strike at Howard & Bullough's, a dispute that was settled only in June, with the loss of some £150,000 in wages. That £150,000 was money from the pockets of people who would probably have spent a little of it at their local Football League club.

Stanley line-up before the opening game of the 1924/25 season. From left to right, back row: Richardson, Watson, Salt, McIntosh, Crawley, Ernest Blackburn (manager). Front row: J. Thompson, Bedford, Mutch, Rooks, R. Thompson, Skillen. A healthy opening day attendance of 7,496 had declined to around 1,000 by the end of the season.

Action from Peel Park during the 1920s. During this bleak period of industrial turmoil, Stanley had to fight hard to survive. Their League record shows a gradual erosion of status as continual waves of financial struggle wore down the morale of the club. From a respectable eighth position in 1923, successive campaigns saw Stanley slip a little further down the rankings: thirteenth, seventeenth, eighteenth, and then, in 1926/27, a desperately poor twenty-first position, with only ten wins all season. Gates dropped alarmingly during this period, sometimes dipping below 2,000, and only a couple of money-spinning cup draws kept the club going. One of these was in January 1926, when Stanley drew Bolton Wanderers at Peel Park. Hopes of a full house were dashed when a police report stated that the ground would be unsafe if filled to capacity. The tie was switched to Burnden Park where Stanley lost 0-1 in front of a 33,000 crowd; this was after their outside-left Walt Gummery had had a goal disallowed and Bolton had been reduced to ten men.

Such was Stanley's fiscal precariousness that whenever the club unearthed a talent, they could rarely afford to reap the fruits of their discovery on the field, nor could they indulge in a gradual process of team building around the better players. Johnny Jepson was a case in point. Drafted in from the reserves in October 1925, Jepson flowered in the first eleven and ended the 1925/26 season with 36 goals from just 33 League and Cup games, including four in Stanley's encouraging run to the final of the Lancashire Senior Cup, where they were defeated 2-5 by Bolton Wanderers. The directors kept hold of Jepson, but did not have the resources to build around him. The following season Jepson struggled terribly in a side that conceded 98 goals on its way to twenty-first position and the ignominy of re-election. Underlining Stanley's misfortunes, they even lost the opportunity to cash in on Jepson's talents when, at the end of the season, the striker opted to sign for non-League Carlisle United, thus ruling out a fee.

In June 1927, the traditional end-of-season Peel Park bring-and-buy sale saw Stanley emerge with a set of players who proved to be good acquisitions, particularly in shoring up a notoriously munificent defence. The prolific form of new striker John Parkin helped Stanley end the 1927/28 season in ninth position. However, gates remained depressed and once again financial pressures were brought to bear upon the medium-term possibilities of nurturing a decent, youthful team at Peel Park. The following season, promising youngsters Chris Dodds and Alf Tootill were sold to Sheffield Wednesday and Wolves, bringing in much-needed revenue but doing nothing to inspire the Accrington public.

In January 1930, Accrington Stanley launched an appeal, but the economic and social conditions were not conducive to fundraising. The Wall Street Crash had depressed Lancashire's cotton export markets. Unemployment in the town stood at 11,700, and many Accringtonians moved away to find work in more prosperous areas. Mr J. Holland, a Stanley director, stood up at a public meeting on 6 January 1930 and underlined the predicament that the club found herself in: 'There is no gainsaying the fact that tonight has got to determine whether Stanley shall go on or go out. The present liabilities of the club are £3,000, and in addition I estimate that we will lose another £1,000 before the end of the season. Therefore the approximate liability we have to face is £4,000. Shall we go on, or shall we give up?'

A wage-trimming scheme submitted to the players was rejected, although they did eventually agree to cuts amounting to some £200. Some connected to the club thought that part-time football was the only option, but there was precious little industrial work around for the players to undertake. Faced with no apparent solution to the vicious cycle of indifferent form and poor gates, the club rescheduled its debts and soldiered on. Ever willing were the club's small band of active supporters, who did the washing and even took the players in during the worst years of the depression. The financial pressures were unceasing, and Stanley continued to sell promising youngsters to whoever made an offer. As townsfolk observed a steady stream of youngsters leave Peel Park, it was perhaps little wonder that gates continued to bump along at an average of 3,000. Results continued to be poor also, the team photo call (above) coming before a 0-5 thrashing at Walsall on 18 November 1933.

Accrington Stanley, October 1934. From left to right, back row: A. Ellison (mascot), Hunter, Gill, Corcoran, McCulloch, Lockie, Clare. Front row: Cull, Harker, Brown, Dodds, Leedham.

During the 1934/35 season, the club sold Joe Clare to Arsenal, Fred Marsden and James Aspin to Wolves, and Fred Leedham to Oldham. These transactions barely wiped out a considerable operating loss of just under £2,000. A turning point of sorts was made in the summer of 1935 when John Hacking, a Blackburnian who kept goal for Oldham, Manchester United and England, was appointed as player-manager.

As if to prove that team-building in part relied on random good fortune, Hacking went to the South Coast to secure one player and just down the road for another, and then found that he had created a potent partnership. Bob Mortimer, an ex-Bolton Wanderers striker, was secured from Bournemouth, whilst winger Georgie Mee, a veteran of five League clubs and 400 League appearances, was signed from Great Harwood. Mortimer was an excellent header of a ball, whilst Mee provided the crosses. It was an unlikely partnership that lifelong Stanley supporter Jack Knowles remembers well: 'Mee was a little fat fellow, but he could centre a ball. Beckham would be a learner compared to Mee! His centres seemed to hang in the air until Mortimer got there. It was a remarkable association. Georgie Mee would get to the byeline and flick it over – he never used to belt it, it just sort of drifted over – and it would hang there and Mortimer would arrive and head it in.'

Hacking soon found life as a Third Division custodian too much, and he retired to concentrate solely on managerial duties. Once the Mee and Mortimer partnership was established, Stanley began to make strides up the League table. However, when Portsmouth came knocking in February 1936 with a cheque for £1,450 for the services of Mortimer and his fellow forward Billy Harker, the club couldn't refuse. Their departure saw Stanley's form decline, but their final League position of ninth was the best for many a year.

The Accrington Stanley team of 1937 that made FA Cup headlines. From left to right, back row: F. Brennand (trainer), Nesbitt, Craven, Gregg, Robertson, Reeday, Andrews, Mee. Front row: Reynolds, Rivers, Mortimer, Pateman, Tyson. Mortimer returned to Stanley early the following season and he soon re-acclimatised to the hanging crosses of Georgie Mee. Up front, Hacking paired Mortimer with Billy Tyson, another astute acquisition from non-League Lancaster City. The signing of the precocious talent of local seventeen-year-old goalkeeper Jack Robinson further strengthened the squad. With these men in place, Stanley embarked on what remains one of their most notable FA Cup adventures. Blessed with the fortune of two home draws against non-League opposition, Stanley progressed to the third round where they drew Blackburn Rovers at Ewood Park. It was a dream tie, and 31,000 spectators saw Mortimer twice put Stanley ahead, only for Blackburn to equalise on both occasions. The replay saw Stanley progress 3-1 after extra-time, with Mortimer once again the hero with another two goals.

A disappointing aspect of the 1937 Cup run was that it did little to convince more people that it was worth spending a Saturday afternoon at Peel Park. The attendance for the Cup replay was nearly 12,000, but at the next League game it was back to the usual 4,000 or so. It wasn't the first time that those connected with the club had voiced their frustration. Five years earlier, Sam Pilkington had warned that Stanley would have to leave the Football League if more support through the turnstiles wasn't forthcoming, but his appeal had been only moderately successful.

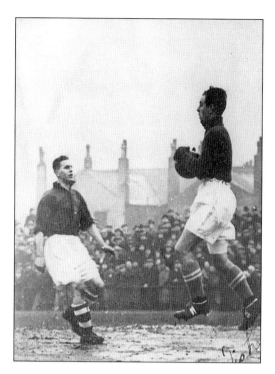

Left: Action from the replay against Blackburn at Peel Park, 20 January 1937. Billy Tyson hovers in the Blackburn penalty area as Rovers' 'keeper Pratt collects the ball. The replay was a huge event in the town, with Accrington's schoolchildren given the afternoon off to watch the game. The FA Cup run of 1936/37 ended at Maine Road, Manchester with a fourth round 0-2 defeat, but the receipts from another 30,000 plus crowd provided some much-needed financial relief.

Right: An Accrington Stanley fixture card; note the patronage of the *Accrington Observer*. With a proven attack, some promising youngsters and money in the bank, Stanley had the basis for a real promotion challenge, but they proved adept at throwing away their good hand. The directors sold the strikers Mortimer and Tyson to Blackburn Rovers just eight games into the 1937/38 season, without lining up replacements. With no proven goalscorers, Stanley sank to the bottom of the League and ultimately had to apply for re-election. This was the end of any possibility of Second Division football before the outbreak of war. All told, the inter-war epoch was a story of the occasional triumph being eked out of continuous hardship and struggle. Accrington Stanley had established themselves as a League club, but one whose viability would occasionally be tested to the limit.

Accrington Stanley F. C.

FIXTURES

for

1938-9

Three

The Land is Ours
1946-1953

Fred Brennand (third from left) was Accrington Stanley's trainer throughout the inter-war period and served under five managers. Teddy Ivill (second from right) played for Stanley between 1935 and 1937 and returned to Peel Park in 1945 as reserve team coach.

In August 1946, Accrington Stanley once more carried the town's standard in the Football League. John Hacking remained at the helm, and two players – Maurice Conroy and Ronald Morgan – remained from the side that had last played League football in 1939. The first season back was disappointing, but a last day 8-4 demolition of Lincoln City heralded better times ahead. This extraordinary game witnessed the debut of a young full-back called Stan Lynn, as well as a hat-trick by mid-season signing Stan Mercer, which brought his final tally to 13 goals from just 19 games.

With Mercer established as the team's centre forward and with a goalscoring inside forward in the shape of Walter Keeley, Stanley began the 1947/48 season on fire, winning five of their first six games. Moreover, the directors of the club went on record saying that Accrington Stanley would no longer sell to survive but would look to maintain high standards among the club's personnel. Unsurprisingly, they failed this resolution at the first hurdle when, in October 1947, Bury arrived at Peel Park with a cheque for £3,500 for the signature of Walter Keeley. To be sure, this was a substantial amount of money, but Keeley was a rare commodity – a goal-scoring winger – and his departure blunted one of the most incisive front lines that Stanley had enjoyed for many a season. The departure of Keeley was one of the factors behind the petering out of the 1947/48 campaign, but the income derived from the sale allowed Stanley to pay off the mortgage on Peel Park. This financial arrangement, made in November 1928, had been possible in the first place only thanks to a loan from Howard & Bullough's. During the 1930s, with the club struggling terribly, the company had twice cancelled scheduled interest payments.

Such was the perceived significance of the full repayment of the mortgage that a celebratory dinner was held in February 1948 at which the deeds of the six acre ground were handed over to the club. It was an opportunity for those who had worked so hard for the club to give each other well-deserved acclaim. The mood of the evening was optimistic. The club's president, W.W. Cocker (*above right*) declared that the club was now on an even keel and that planned improvements would soon make Peel Park a ground 'worthy of football.'

The chairman, Sam Pilkington, gave an altogether more pragmatic analysis. He castigated the level of transfer fees in football, which had reached £20,000, and argued that Stanley must nonetheless cash in if an offer for a player was particularly good. He also stressed the need for Stanley to buy when necessary, but said that he would not allow the club to spend excessively. Despite the sanguine mood of the evening, Pilkington's message was clear and all too familiar: Stanley would sell lucratively but buy cheaply. It was hardly what the fans wanted to hear.

The season of 1948/49 started disastrously, with Stanley unable to register a win until the thirteenth game of the season. One straw in the wind did at least point to the potential that might be harnessed by a successful team. In September, Hull City visited Peel Park with a perfect record of eight straight wins. In the Hull side was the famous Raich Carter, though much attention was also centred on full-back Tom Berry, a native of Clayton-le-Moors. Stanley were defeated 1-2, but the story of the day was the 13,162 crowd, a new League record for Peel Park. However, the season continued in a poor vein and Stanley only just avoided re-election in twentieth place. The only bright spot of the campaign was the prolific form of journeyman striker Don Travis, whose eleven goals in the final twenty-one games of the season hoisted Stanley from the very foot of the table. But the directors decided that manager John Hacking's time was up. He had been at the Peel Park helm for 10 seasons and 14 years, a remarkable record of service during very difficult times.

Stan Lynn (back row, second left) in a Stanley line-up from September 1949. Don Travis is on the far right of the back row.

Jimmy Porter took over for the 1949/50 season, but he was unable to significantly alter the club's fortunes. One player who did benefit from Porter's stewardship was Stan Lynn, a right-back who had made his debut as an eighteen-year-old in the last game of the 1946/47 season. Under Hacking, Lynn was forced to bide his time in the reserves, but Porter soon promoted the young defender and he became a regular first team player. After only a few months in the first team, Lynn became the subject of bids from Newcastle, Birmingham and Aston Villa, the latter offering £4,500. With Stanley's finances in dire straits once more, the offer from Villa represented a lifeline that the club clutched gratefully. One of the most successful Stanley exports, Lynn won the FA Cup and the Second Division title with Aston Villa, and followed this with a 1963 League Cup winners medal in the colours of Birmingham City.

An eight-match run that saw Stanley unbeaten for nearly two months saw them rise to a mid-table position by the end of the 1949/50 season. Six goals in the last five games saw Don Travis reach the 20-goal mark, but few in the town were convinced that the club was on the rise again.

Some Stanley players in pre-season training, August 1950. From left to right, back row: Alick Robinson (trainer), Dennis Smith, Bill Mellor, Paddy Coll, Sam Parker, Eddie Martin, Don Travis. Front row: Joe Slattery, Charlie Hogan, George Rothwell, Fred Martin, Dennis Thomas, Joe Wilson. The season of 1950/51 was an utter disaster from the opening day 0-7 thrashing at Gateshead. The sale of Don Travis to rivals Crewe in November 1950 infuriated the Accrington fans, but they still responded generously to an appeal for transfer money shortly afterwards, helping to raise the £3,000 Stanley paid Liverpool for striker Billy Watkinson in January 1951. Barely six weeks after this ambitious move, manager Jimmy Porter was sacked following a humiliating 1-9 defeat at Lincoln City. He was replaced by Walter Crook, but the new manager had little success. In March 1951, Stanley travelled to Bradford City and were defeated 0-7. It was a game that seemed to sum up Stanley's ill-fortune. They had looked the better side before a couple of opposition challenges reduced them to nine men. With a reshuffled line-up and many players out of position, Bradford ran amok. The *Accrington Observer* could only sympathise: 'The driver pulled his vehicle up, dashed round to the luggage compartment and dragged out the first aid kit. Swabs were needed to staunch the flow of blood. A few minutes later, he did the same thing, this time because there was an inert passenger in need of revival to consciousness. From a nearby house, a kindly soul produced a cup of hot tea. An ambulance on its way from a battlefront? No, just Accrington Stanley on a routine journey home from yet another heartbreak match in this, the blackest season in the club's history. One of these fine days we are going to see a full-strength Stanley go through a match without depleted ranks. Then, if there is poor play and defeat, we can justifiably criticise. But no sane person can have anything else but sympathy both for players and club under circumstances such as operated on Saturday.'

Accrington Stanley, 1950/51. From left to right, back row: D. Smith, J. Wilson, W. Mellor, D. Daniels, F. Martin, R. Webster. Front row: W. Keeley, T. Butler, G. Rothwell, J. Slattery, W. Robinson. Ultimately, Stanley had to apply for re-election, and just 2,782 supporters witnessed the final home game of the season. With attendances so low, it was a surprise to no one that the club posted an operating loss of over £6,000. In the following close season, August 1951, Stanley enrolled the help of the mayor in an effort to generate more sponsorship from local businesses. The *Accrington Observer* leant weight to the campaign, and the town rallied to its football team, with around 9,000 spectators turning out for the first two home games of the season. The visit of Oldham on 6 October actually produced a record League attendance of 13,268. This gate money eased Stanley's financial plight a little, but on the field of play the team continued to struggle desperately. An immediate exit from the FA Cup at the hands of Chester was Stanley's sixth consecutive first round elimination, and the team eventually limped home in twenty-second position, having won just ten league games all season. This abject record made all the more remarkable the performance of striker Billy Watkinson, who managed 22 goals from his 42 starts

By the end of this wretched campaign, finances had once again become a cause for real concern. Stanley director George Pratt set about trying to alleviate the problem with two major initiatives. One was a £4,000 share issue which, although only partially successful, brought some much needed investment into Peel Park. Pratt's other idea, however, was far more innovative, but dragged the club into a controversy that caused huge debate and left some ill feeling.

Councillor Michael Walsh (*right*), seen here in the mayoral robes he wore in 1954, was the representative on Accrington Council who pushed hardest for Pratt's proposal to be accepted.

George Pratt had approached the town Council with a proposition that they buy Peel Park from the club for £10,000 and then lease the ground back at £500 per year, equivalent to a 5% return on the investment. The proposal was enthusiastically talked up by the fans throughout the summer of 1952. Though the Council considered the matter seriously, they eventually rejected the proposal. However, with the issue now the talk of the town, Councillor Walsh tabled an amendment that sought to reverse this recommendation. A petition urging the Council to reconsider was signed by over a thousand people, and a letter to the *Accrington Observer* put the case succinctly: 'It is a serious matter to the town itself which is so well known, not only in this country but throughout the world, simply because of its football club. The loan to the Football Club won't cost the ratepayers anything and would provide better interest than the Corporation at present receive. As a tradesman in the town coming into contact with all classes of our townsmen and women, there is not the slightest doubt that they are in positive favour, and are trusting the Council will sanction this loan and help us retain what is our most valuable town asset and sport.'

On the night of the vote – 2 September 1952 – Councillor Walsh made an impassioned plea to his fellow councillors, two of whom were also Stanley shareholders and who therefore declined to vote. Those omissions were vital. The amendment was rejected by thirteen votes to twelve. This was a bitter blow for the leaders of the club. Chairman Sam Pilkington reacted diplomatically, remarking 'I really don't know what we shall do now. The whole position looks extremely black for the club.'

The Football League long service medal (*above*) awarded to Stanley secretary Jack Wigglesworth in 1952. It was no coincidence that the only football medals that came to Peel Park at this time were commemorative ones. As deserved as such accolades were, the signing of thirty-seven-year-old Syd Goodfellow in the close season of the 1952/53 campaign underlined Stanley's position. For the professional footballer, Stanley had become a club of last resort, a wretched state of affairs underlined by defeat in ten of their first thirteen League games. Morale was almost non-existent, and any remaining Peel Park atmosphere evaporated as crowds dwindled. A first round pairing with non-League Horden Colliery at least gave Stanley the opportunity to break their post-war FA Cup duck, and this they did with a narrow 2-1 victory. But normal service was resumed in the second round with a 0-2 home defeat at the hands of Mansfield Town.

With only six league victories from thirty-one games, and with Stanley anchored firmly to the bottom of the division, Walter Crook resigned in February 1953. With no immediate replacement forthcoming, the directors picked the team for the rest of the season. Stanley finished well adrift, having won only 8 games in total and taken just 4 points from 23 fixtures away from home. Thanks to the influence of Sam Pilkington, another trial by re-election was successfully negotiated.

Once more, Accrington Stanley had failed to build on the potential afforded by possession of players like Mercer, Keeley and Lynn, and by the security of ground ownership. By the end of the 1952/53 season, there were few players of any value in the squad, and relations with the Council, hitherto mutually beneficial, were tarnished by the controversy over the purchase of Peel Park. Club chairman Sam Pilkington decided to step down, and first-team trainer Billy Wrigglesworth left to take up an appointment elsewhere. The club, still without a manager, also had to contend with a disillusioned townsfolk who were increasingly inclined to stay away from Peel Park altogether. Things could hardly have been less promising as a young, dapper Scotsman arrived in Accrington in the summer of 1953, having accepted the position of player-manager. Promotion to the Second Division was absurd to contemplate, but Walter Galbraith had other ideas.

Four

The Caledonian
Connection
1953-1958

Walter Galbraith, as player-manager, with his first Stanley team. From left to right, back row: B. Jones, J. Cadden, H. Bodle, W. Mellor, W. White, K. Holliday. Front row: L. Cocker, J. Devlin, Galbraith, H. Eastham, D. Musgrave. Walter Galbraith emerged as the successful candidate only after approaches to high-profile players like Manchester United's Johnny Carey and Newcastle's Joe Harvey had failed. Galbraith's previous venture into management at New Brighton had been a singular failure, but the Stanley board was impressed with Galbraith's character and attitude, though he was given just a one-year contract. Galbraith was under no illusions about the financial situation at Peel Park, and the role of club treasurer George Pratt was crucial. Pratt was a strong presence on the board, a man for whom debt was a four-letter word but who was also willing to listen and accept ideas from all quarters if he thought the club would benefit. It was Pratt who oversaw the repayment of the Players' Loan Fund and a substantial reduction in Stanley's long-term debt by the end of the 1952/53 season. In an interview in May 1953, Pratt revealed that an offer from Port Vale for striker Billy Watkinson would have allowed the club to break even for the 1952/53 campaign. Unusually, the club turned down the offer, in part due to Pratt's cautiously optimistic outlook towards the club's finances and fortunes. 'If the efforts which are being made now develop properly, I think we shall start the new season with greatly enhanced financial prospects. If we do not have any bad luck – and we have had more than our share – we may be able to put some money on one side to build up and buy the sort of players we need to make progress in the League with a first-rate team.'

Just a few weeks later, George Pratt was made chairman of Accrington Stanley, and the summer weeks that followed were ones of furious industry that belied the club's lowly status and indicated a new sense of purpose. Galbraith embarked on a radical programme of team building, recruiting many fellow Scots to the Peel Park ranks, and Harry Hubbick was confirmed as the new first-team trainer. To add to the sense of renewal, a band of supporters constructed the rows of terracing that became the Peel Park Kop at the Huncoat side of the ground, increasing the ground capacity to just short of 20,000.

It's a well worn maxim that genuine progress often requires unrealistic expectations to get the whole process moving, but Pratt and Galbraith dampened excessive hopes, fearing that they would burden rather than energise. Yet the transformation at the club in the space of just a few months was remarkable. Accrington Stanley began preparations for the 1953/54 season with a new chairman, manager and trainer, all with new ideas and fresh ambitions. At the club AGM in August 1953, the chairman argued that consolidation both on and off the field was the aim of the new regime, and that new signings were part of the plan: 'We are aiming to make absolutely certain we are not anywhere near those last two places, and we shall be very disappointed if we are less than half way. We shall be tying ourselves up financially, but on the other hand we shall be entitled to regard them as a good investment for the future.'

Walter Galbraith exuded an air of realistic confidence: 'The lads are new and have to get to know each other. I would like to call upon supporters to be patient and given them all the encouragement they can. I am quite sure the lads will respond. I am very confident indeed that Accrington Stanley will be in a very favourable position at the end of the season.'

Plans for a new stand (above) along the Burnley Road side of the ground were unveiled shortly after the commencement of the season. Mr E. Walne (above left) puts the finishing touches to a model of the proposed construction, watched by Charles Kilby. By the eve of the new season, Galbraith had spent a record amount of money on new players. One headline in the *Accrington Observer* noted that Stanley would field a practically new team, and the paper could not help but be impressed by the pedigree of the new players and the collective spirit around the club: 'Despite all the heartbreaks and travail which should teach Stanleyites the dangers of building castles in the sky, the old spirit is there. The spirit of the new men – and the retained players, too – is remarkable. There is a zest for training which I have seldom seen before. Their enthusiasm is well matched by Walter Galbraith, himself getting in top trim, and by the chairman, who has spent most of his non-business waking hours at the ground.'

The scheme which perhaps underlined the new enterprise at the club most clearly was the proposal, put forward by the chairman, to install floodlights at Peel Park (pictured above, shortly after installation). With the backing of the board confirmed, Pratt went to the media a few days before the opening game of the season and secured front page headlines with his announcement that Peel Park would be one of the first football grounds in the country with permanent floodlighting. He also took the opportunity to appeal to the Accrington public for their support during the forthcoming season. It was a canny piece of publicity, designed to heighten the perception that Accrington Stanley was a club going places.

Both the chairman and the manager may have been disappointed with an opening day crowd of below 10,000, but what was instantly noticeable was that Accrington Stanley were now attempting to play a flowing, passing style of football. That the team needed time to perfect their system was obvious, but the *Accrington Observer* was more optimistic about the immediate impression of Galbraith's Stanley, enthusing as unfamiliar names like Cocker, Bodle, Eastham and Devlin attacked with style and speed. Stockport County were dispatched 2-1 in that opening game, but Galbraith's Stanley found away wins difficult to come by. A 3-0 success at Crewe was a rarity in that it brought a clean sheet away from home. More typical was the 4-6 defeat at Bradford Park Avenue, followed soon after by a 3-5 defeat at Southport.

Stanley's final 1953/54 position of fifteenth was perhaps slightly disappointing, but outweighing this was the obvious air of renewal and progress at Peel Park. Harold Bodle (*left*) played throughout the season. His rather conservative demeanour off the pitch made an odd contrast to his ferocious competitiveness on it. Bodle was very quickly established as a Peel Park favourite.

Right: A portrait of Armour Ashe, drawn by young Stanley fan Maureen Neville. Ashe was signed in October 1953 as Galbraith searched for more defensive coherence. He was new to English League football, having had an unsuccessful trial with Stockport County, who brought him south from St Mirren. Misfortune struck Stanley with the serious injury of striker Ian Brydon, signed from Darlington in October. His partnership with Les Cocker was looking particularly promising, but he suffered a broken leg at Halifax just eight games into his Accrington career and was sidelined for three months.

TEAMS
ACCRINGTON STANLEY

Jones

2 Holliday   3 Ashe

4 Bodle   5 Ryden   6 Sneddon

7 Devlin   8 Cocker   9 Brydon   10 Eastham   11 Musgrave

Referee :   Linesmen :

Mr. H. P. Hartley
Nelson   (RED FLAG)

(YELLOW FLAG)

11 Ring   10 Baird   9 Hill   8 Robb   7 Buchanan

6 Keogh   5 Murphy, E.   4 Anderson

3 Ferrier   2 Murphy, A.

Watson
CLYDE

In January 1954, Stanley proudly unveiled their new floodlights and announced that a forthcoming reserve team game would be used to test the lights and focus them in the right areas of the pitch. An amazing 5,000 spectators turned out on a freezing night to witness the new technology at work. With this experiment successfully completed, Stanley finalised arrangements for a series of evening floodlit friendlies with Scottish League teams, the manager making the most of his Caledonian connections.

The first of these nighttime confrontations with the Celts was on February 15, when Stanley were hosts to East Fife in a game that served as the 'official' unveiling of the floodlights. A week later, Third Lanark made the journey south of the border. Stanley emerged victorious from both games, but more important was the emphatic endorsement of the Accrington public for floodlit football, with around 10,000 people attending both games, providing welcome additional income. The third floodlit friendly took place in early April, with 6,200 turning out for the visit of Clyde. That Stanley made the effort to produce matchday programmes (above) for even these fixtures demonstrates how the club were alive to the need to maximise revenue from what was bound to be a short-term fad.

In the League, a poor run in the new year brought back fears that the club might once more sink into the re-election battle. An anonymous letter in the *Accrington Observer* criticised the chairman's emphasis on clearing debt to the detriment of the team. 'Surely the creditors would not object to waiting a little longer. The primary object should be the team. It is of little use expecting the manager to go to Scotland with the price of a packet of cigarettes, and expecting to buy George Young and Charlie Tully. He has certainly made a good job of his limited allowance, but he cannot be expected to always be so fortunate.'

Pratt responded strongly to this criticism, pointing out that the manager had never been refused money for a player. The chairman also denied that Galbraith had been 'lucky' with his purchases, arguing instead that any reward had been the fruition of many hours of scouting and networking.

In one week of February 1954, Galbraith completed the signings of centre half John Ryden (above left) and goalkeeper Jimmy Jones (above right). It took a £1,000 cheque to convince Alloa Athletic to sell Ryden, of whom Galbraith had long been an admirer. The manager's judgement was soon vindicated as a host of top clubs eyed the young centre half enviously. Ryden went straight into the Stanley first team and helped his new club to mid-table respectability, exactly the position for which Galbraith and Pratt had aimed.

In virtually every respect, the 1953/54 season had been a pleasant success. Gate receipts were up by fifty per cent, enabling the club to clear long-standing, depletive debts. Stanley had the summer wage money in the bank by Easter, enabling them to keep the squad together. The Supporters' Club, ever resourceful, raised £17,000 over the course of the season through an innovative football pools scheme. Without a doubt, the sorry fortunes of Accrington Stanley had been transformed in a matter of months, and Walter Galbraith was rewarded with a new and lucrative contract. The *Accrington Observer* summed it up with their headline on the season's review: 'Chance to build bright future on memorable season'. The local paper was in no doubt that Galbraith had the nucleus of a great side. 'With the addition of two or three tip top men to strengthen positions, there is no reason why Stanley should not vie with the best in the Section, and indeed be challenging. That is a dream which looked to be impossible twelve months ago with a mere handful of retained players and a weight of debt that was pressing down cruelly. What a change has taken place! Credit must go in full measure to the people who have made it all possible from the Chairman, Mr G.A. Pratt, his board, manager, trainer, officials, players and the many stout-hearted helpers. No more is Stanley a 'Cinderella' club, but an organisation that counts in the soccer world.'

Les Cocker (left) and Archie Wright. In the close season of the 1954/55 campaign, Galbraith unveiled the signings that he hoped would provide additional strength in depth and take Stanley the extra mile to promotion. Wing-half Eddie Hunter went straight into the first team, while new goalkeeper Tom McQueen provided real competition for Jimmy Jones. Another important signing was that of Archie Wright, who formed a prolific inside forward partnership with Les Cocker. Wright had cost Blackburn Rovers £10,000 when they signed him from Falkirk in May 1951, but he had struggled to establish a regular first team place. Les Cocker was a complete footballer, able to play with both feet, as well as being a good tackler and header of the ball. Stanley also set Cocker on the road to further glory as a coach. In May 1957, he was appointed assistant trainer at Peel Park and gained the training and coaching qualifications that saw him eventually assist Alf Ramsey in the triumphant 1966 World Cup campaign. Cocker also served Don Revie, both as club coach at Leeds and as assistant during Revie's tenure as England manager.

In November 1954, Cocker produced a memorable performance in the Lancashire Senior Cup, scoring a hat-trick against an Everton team that included future Burnley manager Harry Potts. Stanley won the game 3-2.

ACCRINGTON STANLEY F.C. (1921) LTD.

Stand **B**

FLOODLIT MATCH

Accrington   Stanley

v.

Everton

1st NOVEMBER, 1954
Kick-off 7-30 p.m.

4/- including tax

Row **D**

Seat **9**

The much-awaited 1954/55 season opened with an anti-climactic 1-1 draw at home to Southport in front of 11,293 spectators. However, Stanley soon settled down and a 4-0 home win against Oldham on 8 September was a fourth straight victory. The line-up above was for Stanley's next fixture, at Mansfield, on 11 October 1954. From left to right, back row: Holliday, Ashe, Jones, Hunter, Ryden, Bodle. Front row: Devlin, Wright, Watkinson, Cocker, Scott. The hero of the Oldham game was Watkinson, who had scored a rapid hat-trick. Just a week later he was sold to Halifax Town, seemingly without a replacement being brought in. Unsurprisingly, voices of consternation were raised, but Galbraith knew exactly what he was doing.

George Stewart (*above*) was Galbraith's target. The striker was registered with St Mirren but playing for Worcester City, and fees to both clubs secured the player's signature. Stewart was to have a profound impact at Peel Park.

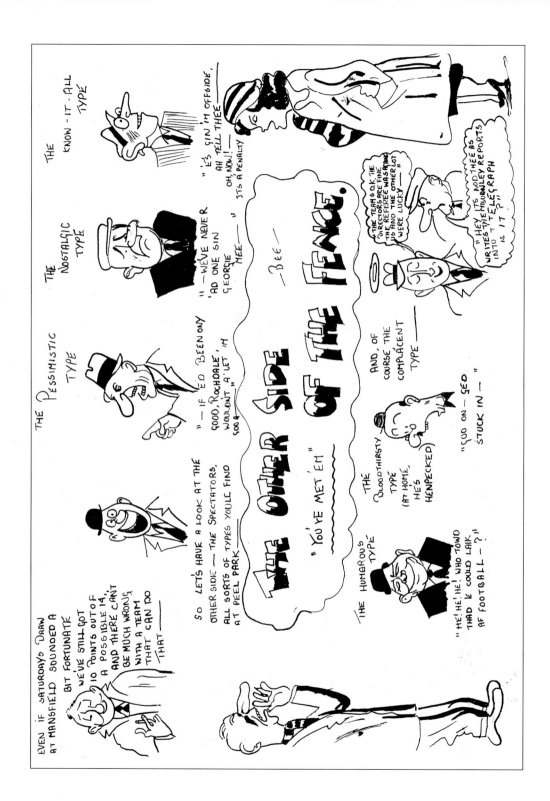

The purchase of Jimmy Harrower in December 1954 was another decisive move by Walter Galbraith that was looked upon as the final piece in the Stanley jigsaw. Harrower filled the left-back berth, Armour Ashe was moved to right-back, and the central trio of Eddie Hunter, John Ryden and Harold Bodle completed the defensive line. With Harrower on board, Stanley embarked on a superb unbeaten run that included seven straight League victories through the New Year period.

Despite the manifest improvements under Galbraith, the perceived fickleness of the Stanley faithful was still evident, certainly in the eyes of Tom Booth at any rate. Under the pseudonym of 'Bee', Booth published booklets of cartoons and stories about his beloved Accrington Stanley. Although he was a dedicated fan, Booth viewed the Board with suspicion and was often critical of his fellow supporters. The cartoon above depicts two supporters walking home from a dour 1-0 defeat of Bradford City on 29 January 1955, Stanley's sixth of their seven consecutive victories. The two are all too ready to grumble at the team's performance until results elsewhere prove the victory to be a vital one.

Left: Tom Booth's hilarious study of Peel Park regulars, published after the 2-2 draw at Mansfield, October 1954.

The line-up seen by many as the greatest Accrington Stanley side. From left to right, back row: Walter Galbraith (manager), Jimmy Harrower, Eddie Hunter, Armour Ashe, Tom McQueen, Harold Bodle, John Ryden, Charlie Sneddon, Harry Hubbick (trainer). Front row: Joe Devlin, Les Cocker, George Stewart, Archie Wright, Bert Scott.

The visit of Tranmere Rovers on 26 March attracted only 5,200 spectators, this at a time when Stanley were challenging strongly for promotion. This prompted an appeal in the *Accrington Observer*, whose headline reminded the townsfolk that 'Spectators, too, have their part to play in Reds' promotion bid'. Chairman Pratt told the paper: 'We were bitterly disappointed at the attendance last Saturday. I am quite certain that some thousands went to watch the Burnley-Wolves match from Accrington, and if people in the town prefer to do that sort of thing, then how can we expect to have Second Division football? Spectators play as big a part as anyone in the success of a club.'

He ended the interview with an appeal to the Accrington public: 'We have not yet broken a ground record in a League match this season. Surely we are entitled to that in this wonderful season. There is no reason why we should not have 15,000 to watch York City here on Easter Monday. It can easily be done and people as a result can show us they wish us well in our fight to give them Second Division football.' The Accrington public responded to the call, and a new League attendance record of 15,425 came through the turnstiles on the Easter Monday, this despite a disastrous 2-5 home defeat to Hartlepool on the Saturday which had dented Stanley's promotion hopes. The throng witnessed a 2-2 draw, and though Stanley rallied with three wins in their last four games, it was not enough to prevent Barnsley from taking the title and the all-important promotion into the Second Division.

Accrington Stanley Reserves, 1954/55. From left to right, back row: Walter Taylor (trainer), Peter Dunne, Gordon Stones, Jimmy Jones, Charlie Ferguson, Ken Holliday, Jimmy Hinksman. Front row: Lever, Jackie Currie, Tommy McKeown, Harry Eastham, Tommy Henderson. The success of Stanley's reserve side, who battled to a brilliant Lancashire Combination League and Cup double, underlines the progress made by the club under Galbraith and Pratt. In the line-up is a youthful Jimmy Hinksman, one of the few local players to serve Stanley at this time. Hinksman would go on to be a major figure in the resurrection of Accrington Stanley in the late 1960s and early '70s.

Galbraith was keen to stress that well-earned laurels would not be rested upon. After a 3-0 victory at Bradford had concluded the 1954/55 season and guaranteed Stanley the runners-up position, Galbraith told the press: 'My plans for next season are already in operation. I am now in the position at which I aimed when I took over here and I think I can build still further, chiefly from young players. I am, in fact, highly confident about next season and I believe there is no reason why we should not do equally as well, if not a little better.'

Stanley's rise in the football world was appreciated beyond the locality. In the programme for the final game at Bradford, a writer commented that: 'Stanley's rise from the lower regions of the Northern Section to become promotion challengers is one of the most gripping and romantic of the season'. But in football, romance is one thing, results entirely another.

Just a few of the 10,000 Accrington fans who made the journey to Anfield for a third round FA Cup tie against Liverpool in January 1956. Galbraith's Stanley once again challenged for promotion throughout the 1955/56 season. When, in March 1956, the Reds came from two goals down to beat Scunthorpe 3-2 away from home, Stanley were second to Grimsby Town only on goal difference and had a game in hand. However, a loss of form towards the end of the season cost the club dearly. Only one win from the final five games saw Stanley lose out once more, finishing third behind Derby County and Grimsby. Another misfortune was an article in a Sunday newspaper that revealed the success of the Supporters' Club's football pools scheme. Since football pools were technically illegal at this time, the scheme was run independently by Stanley fan Albert Lucas and a team of volunteers who sold thousands of tickets in factories and workplaces throughout the town. But it was common knowledge that the profits went to Accrington Stanley, and in two years this unofficial operation raised a huge £30,000 for the club. This money was central to Stanley's ability to pay good wages and retain their squad. Due to the publicity from the media, the scheme was suspended and a valuable source of income cut off.

Asked for his opinion as to why the Reds had once more stumbled at the final hurdle in the quest for promotion, chairman Pratt cited a lack of strength in depth. 'If we have learned one lesson from this season it is that before an attempt can be made on promotion, one must have an adequate reserve of playing strength. We have not had that reserve strength for the simple reason that we could not afford it. There was only one other club in the Third Division that had a smaller number of professional players than we had. We are determined to put that right in the coming season.'

Just one month after making this determined statement, George Pratt tendered his resignation as chairman, and although he would eventually stay on, it was the first crack to publicly appear in the Galbraith-Pratt partnership.

Right: the Liverpool FA Cup tie remains one of the most famous occasions in the history of Accrington Stanley. It gave the players the opportunity to play in front of nearly 50,000 spectators. They performed with distinction, maintaining their passing game and matching Liverpool for style and flair, but two sublime moments of skill from Billy Liddell created match-winning opportunities. The game demonstrated that Stanley were as good a footballing side as most Second Division teams, and convinced many at the club that the team would be able to compete at the higher level.

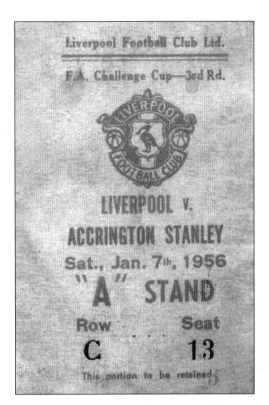

Liverpool Football Club Ltd.

F.A. Challenge Cup—3rd Rd.

LIVERPOOL v.
ACCRINGTON STANLEY
Sat., Jan. 7th, 1956
"A" STAND
Row   Seat
C   13

This portion to be retained

Left: Les Cocker, Harold Bodle and Armour Ashe. The 1956/57 season saw a gradual but inevitable break-up of Galbraith's first Stanley squad, which had done so much to raise the profile and self-esteem of the club. Harold Bodle, signed by Galbraith in August 1953, made his last appearance on 1 September 1956, in a 3-3 home draw with Mansfield. He was by this time thirty-seven years old and had been troubled with injuries. Other established first team players like Joe Devlin, Archie Wright, Norrie McCreadie and Les Cocker also found that injuries and loss of form limited their first-team opportunities.

ON STANLEY ON

The Official Organ of Accrington Stanley Supporters' Association

| No. 1 Vol. 1. | APRIL, 1956 | Price Twopence |

Contributed by G. A. PRATT, Chairman of the
Stanley Board of Directors

I welcome this new venture of the Supporters' Association. For one thing, it is very practical evidence that they are far from losing their enthusiasm and initiative. For another, it gives us still another opportunity of letting our true supporters know what is going on in the world of Accrington Stanley. This magazine is a tribute to the initiative and imagination of the Committee, and their indefatigable secretary, Albert Lucas. Modest as its beginnings may now be, it may soon grow to an organ truly representative of the spirit of endeavour which animates all sections of our Club's activities. I hope that through its columns every reader of this little magazine will grow to feel that he is one of a team of enthusiasts, and will join with us in our common endeavour to further the progress of our town's Club. With such united effort there is no limit to what we can do. If we are truly " all for one and one for all " success is bound to crown our efforts, and we shall be able to point with pride to our achievements.

SUCCESS TO THE MAGAZINE AND TO THE
SUPPORTERS' ASSOCIATION.

50

Tom McQueen (*left*) and Bill McInnes, August 1956. Halfway through the 1956/57 season, highly-rated goalkeeper Tom McQueen left Accrington Stanley for personal reasons and returned to Scotland. Fortunately for Stanley, waiting in the wings was another Scot, Bill McInnes. He had been McQueen's understudy during the previous season and had made his debut at a difficult time when points were desperately needed to stay in the promotion frame. Galbraith had no hesitation in handing the green jersey to McInnes, and an improvement in form during March and early April saw Stanley once again challenge for promotion. However, McInnes was badly injured at Gateshead on 13 April, and his absence told as Stanley faltered in the final few games that they had to win in order to secure promotion.

Left: the Supporters' Club was a highly active and effective group. In February 1957, they issued a pamphlet that revealed they had contributed £35,294 to the club in five years. This caused something of a stir in the town, and the board issued some figures of their own to show where the money had gone. Such had been the increase in costs that Stanley had an average shortfall of around £7,000 per year, even when increased gate receipts were taken into account. The wage bill had risen from £12,000 per year in 1953 to £18,250 in 1956. Commenting on these figures, the *Accrington Observer* noted that the £6,250 in additional wages was the difference between a poor, struggling side at the foot of the table and one with good players that could take the club into the Second Division.

Hull City *v*. Accrington Stanley, 19 April 1957. Peter Sowden is about to challenge for a high ball in the Hull goalmouth at Boothferry Park during Stanley's desperate search for promotion points. This game ended in a narrow 1-2 defeat and was the first of three end-of-season reversals that put paid to Stanley's promotion hopes. For the second consecutive season, Stanley finished third – their third consecutive top-three finish. Some commentators blamed lost home points, but the reality was that Stanley's challenge had once again been found just short of what was required to win a very tough and hard fought division. On the positive side, new attacking players like Jimmy Anders and Jimmy Mulkerrin were brought to Peel Park, and Galbraith continued his search for the players who would finally bring the elusive promotion that Stanley undoubtedly deserved.

Accrington Stanley, 1957/58. From left to right, back row: Mulkerrin, Ashe, McInnes, Dick, Tighe. Middle row: L. Cocker (assistant trainer), Sneddon, Stones, Scott, Ralston, Hunter, H. Hubbick (trainer). Front row: Sowden, Anders, Harrower, W. Galbraith (manager), Pirie, Stewart, McNichol.

The 1957/58 campaign saw Stanley challenging for promotion for the fourth successive season, but once again they narrowly missed out on the big prize of Second Division football, finishing the season as runners-up to Scunthorpe United. The frustration of yet another near miss was compounded by other factors that seemed to indicate that Stanley were almost destined to struggle. The fixture schedule had seen every Stanley home game in competition with either Burnley or Blackburn, both First Division clubs. Predictably, Stanley's average attendance at Peel Park fell for the fourth consecutive season, with the loss of revenue calculated at around £1,000. Promotion to the Second Division would have given Stanley full membership of the Football League, and with it the right to negotiate fixtures with their neighbours on an equal standing. Neither could the club rely on floodlit friendlies to make up the cash shortfall as they had done in the past. Most League clubs now possessed floodlights, leaving night-time football with little of the novelty that had initially attracted curious crowds.

Perhaps most significantly, this last failure to achieve promotion heralded Stanley's last effort in the Third Division (North). The Football League Management Committee had finally managed to convince the clubs to approve the abolition of regional football and the institution of nationwide Third and Fourth Divisions. This arrangement would clearly favour the bigger Southern sides, but as runners-up in the Northern Section, Stanley secured their place in the Third Division for the season of 1958/59.

ACCRINGTON STANLEY

McInnes

2 McNicol   3 Harrower

4 Tighe   5 Kelly   6 Sneddon

Scott   8 Mulkerrin   9 Stewart   10 Dick   11 Anders, H

Referee :

Mr. E. S. Oxley,
Pontefract.

Linesmen :

Mr. A. Edge,
Liverpool.
(Red Flag)

Mr. C. Evans,
Timperley.
(Yellow Flag)

11 Ormerod   10 Birch   9 Purdon   8 Gray   7 Co

6 King   5 Roberts   4 Procter

3 Jackson   2 Fraser

Coglin

BARROW

The teams for Walter Galbraith's final home game as manager of Accrington Stanley, Thursday 24 April 1958. As Stanley prepared for the 1958/59 season and nationwide Third Division football – with vastly increased travel and administration costs to account for – the Board summoned Galbraith to a meeting. They asked him to agree to certain economies in the light of operating losses that amounted to £10,000 over the previous two seasons. Galbraith refused to co-operate with the plans and offered his resignation, which was accepted by the Board. It was a regrettable end to a reign which had cajoled and inspired the club into hitherto uncharted territory. The last word on the Galbraith era goes to Jack Knowles – 'We never hoofed the ball anywhere with Galbraith. We always played good football. We were the best footballing side by a mile. My father had watched football since before the First World War at Burnley and Blackburn, and he'd gone down to London to watch Arsenal and Chelsea, he'd watched Liverpool and Everton. And he told me that this Accrington Stanley side was the best footballing team that had ever played in the Third Division. But we were never tough enough to win the League. The teams that won were like Barnsley – very big, tough and physical sides. Good football alone doesn't win you games, you need that little bit extra, that bit of bite. But we'd some good days with Galbraith, the best days, in fact.'

Five

The Price of the Ticket
1958-1962

Action from Stanley's FA Cup Second Round tie *v*. Buxton, 6 December 1958.

The departure of Walter Galbraith may not have been entirely unexpected – in March 1958 he had been linked with a managerial vacancy at First Division Blackpool – but the suddenness of his leaving, so close to the start of such a challenging new season, astonished many Stanley supporters. It was perhaps fortunate that Stanley, and their new manager George Eastham, could rely on a midfield stalwart like Charlie Sneddon (above left), starting his sixth season at Peel Park. Harvey McCreadie (above right) was one of Galbraith's last signings for Accrington Stanley, and in February 1959 he became the youngest player to appear for Accrington Stanley in a Football League match, aged just 16 years and 143 days.

Left: Another reliable braveheart of the Stanley squad was right-back Bob McNichol, seen here on the right with new first-team colleague Graham Lord. Unusually for a Galbraith signing, Graham Lord was a local lad, which is perhaps the reason for the English bulldog mascot. The emergence of youngsters like Lord and McCreadie, coupled with a solid start to the Third Division campaign, suggested that life after Galbraith might not be as arduous as expected.

Stanley line-up early in the 1958/59 season. From left to right, back row: T. Tighe, B. McNichol, G. Stones, B. McInnes, J. Harrower, C. Sneddon. Front row: H. Anders, B. Scott, G. Stewart, W. Dick, J. Anders. In November 1958, an emphatic 5-1 defeat of Workington in the first round of the FA Cup was overshadowed by the departure the following week of centre forward George Stewart, who was sold to Fourth Division Coventry City for £3,500. After 136 League goals in 182 appearances, he left the club as the most prolific goalscorer to have ever graced Peel Park. His single strike in the win over Workington was his 152nd and last goal in the colours of Accrington Stanley.

A Stanley effort flies narrowly wide of the Workington goal. The club had been given permission to seat 1,000 spectators in the new Burnley Road stand before it had been finished, and this cup-tie was scheduled to be the first game at which all 2,300 seats could be sold. From the evidence of this photograph, there was still some work to be done.

Two Bert Scott goals from the 1958/59 FA Cup competition that saw Stanley make a rare excursion to the last thirty-two. *Above:* Scott completes his hat-trick in the Workington tie. *Below:* Scott rises to head in one of his two goals in Stanley's 6-1 second round defeat of non-League Buxton. Another home draw in the third round saw Stanley progress at the expense of Darlington. In the fourth round Stanley were paired at home to First Division Portsmouth, and in front of 12,395 they forced a 0-0 draw before losing 1-4 in the replay. Stanley forward Wattie Dick (10), rejoined Walter Galbraith at Bradford Park Avenue just a fortnight after the Buxton game.

Left: Some Stanley players relax before the Portsmouth Cup tie. From top: Bob McNichol, Terry Tighe, Alex Hamilton, Hugh Stinson, Jimmy Mulkerrin. Walter Galbraith signed Jimmy Mulkerrin, a Scottish 'B' international, as an inside forward, a position from which he managed a prolific scoring rate. Mulkerrin was assigned the almost impossible task of replacing George Stewart as the team's No. 9 and main goalscorer.

On 17 January 1959, Accrington took to a frozen Peel Park for a League fixture against Swindon Town. After thirty-six minutes, and with Stanley leading 1-0 through a Terry Tighe goal, the referee called the game off. Here, Bert Scott (8) challenges for a cross in the Swindon goalmouth.

An Accrington forward, possibly one of the Anders brothers, heads for goal as Stanley take on champions elect of the Third Division Plymouth Argyle at a very wet Peel Park, on 25 April 1959. Terry Tighe's ninth goal of the season secured a point in a 1-1 draw. Stanley's line-up that afternoon in what was the penultimate game of the season was significantly different from the one that had started in August. Gone were players of the calibre of George Stewart, Bill McNichol, and Wattie Dick. They had all been sold to address debts and reduce the wage bill, and the fortunes of the team suffered as a consequence. The Stanley player seen in the background is Sid Storey, then thirty-nine years old and best remembered for his part in York City's run to the FA Cup semi-finals in 1955. Stanley were not helped by a severe injury crisis during the second half of 1958/59, but there was a feeling around Peel Park that the momentum built up under Galbraith was dissipating quickly.

The *Accrington Observer* sensed this too, and ran a piece highlighting the dangers of falling support. Club vice-president Sam Pilkington suggested a public meeting between club officials and supporters so that both could air their opinions and move forward together. Manager George Eastham bluntly declared that: 'We don't want supporters who go to Burnley one week, Blackburn the next and only come to Peel Park occasionally'. But Stanley weren't in a position to turn down any kind of support, and Sam Pilkington's tone was more diplomatic. 'Unless there is a considerable improvement, Stanley will be in the gravest danger of sinking into the Fourth Division. The people who have so obviously stayed away ought to be invited to say just why they have done so. Only in that way can we sort things out.'

Stanley still had a nucleus of a good team that had beaten the best in the division, witnessed by fine 4-2 victories at Plymouth and Norwich. They had also earned a classy 2-1 victory at Swindon, a team who had been undefeated in their previous nineteen League games. However, if the core of a good team remained, there were also signs that the squad as a whole was in real need of reinforcement. As the 1958/59 season petered out, Stanley were hammered 2-5 at Bournemouth, 0-9 at Tranmere and 0-5 at Reading.

Another problem for Stanley was the revival in fortunes of their League neighbours. Blackburn Rovers had just completed their first season back in the First Division, and Stanley had been given permission to play League games on Friday night as a means of combating the pulling power of local First Division football. The experiment was first tried on 12 September 1958 when Brentford were the visitors, and a healthy 9,918 crowd supported the venture. A month later, Stanley played Southend on a Friday night so they could avoid a clash with a Blackburn-Burnley derby.

A statistically improbable occurrence as Jimmy and Harry Anders both celebrate the arrival of twins in early 1959. The Anders brothers were consistent performers on the wings for Stanley, with Jimmy (right) ending the 1958/59 season as top scorer, with 20 League and Cup goals – quite an achievement for a winger.

A pre-season line-up, August 1959, with trainer Harry Hubbick. From left to right, back row: Vincent Jack, Charlie Sneddon, Ken Garrity. Middle row: Marsden, Bill Brown, Graham Lord, Harvey McCreadie, Jimmy Harrower, Eric Jones, Lawson Bennett. Front row: Terry Tighe, Jimmy Anders, Jackie Keeley, Harry Anders, Bill McInnes.

George Eastham resigned as Accrington Stanley manager in June 1959. Harold Bodle, captain of the great 1954/55 side and a Peel Park favourite, was the popular appointment as the new manager. Financial restraints saw the club accept a £3,000 fee for Jimmy Mulkerrin, and the loss of young talent Ian Gibson left Stanley with precious few forward options. Gibson was a Stanley amateur who had been tempted to Bradford Park Avenue in highly dubious circumstances by none other than Walter Galbraith, who was now Bradford's manager. Stanley took the issue to the League Management Committee, but the transfer was ultimately deemed to be above board, though Stanley remained adamant that the player had been illegally poached. Bodle moved to strengthen his forward line and made a number of new signings, but few came with any real pedigree. Inside forward Jackie Keeley seemed to be an exception, signed from First Division Everton and with England Youth caps to his name. He cost Stanley a considerable fee at a time when cash was desperately short and no doubt great things were expected of him. Perhaps illustrating Stanley's luck at this time, Keeley was dropped after just ten League games, clearly uninterested in playing for Accrington.

Two action shots from Stanley's 0-0 draw with Reading at Peel Park, 28 September 1959. *Above:* Jackie Keeley (8) challenges the Reading keeper in what was his last game for Stanley at Peel Park. *Below:* A run and shot from Bodle's other signing, Eric Jones, flies just wide of the post. Like Keeley, Jones had cost Stanley money when there were precious few resources available. Signed as an inside forward, he never settled into what was a struggling team and failed to score in eighteen League games before moving to Southport at the end of the season.

Stanley manager Harold Bodle (right) signs Harvey McCreadie as a full-time professional on 6 October 1959, just five days after McCreadie's seventeenth birthday. On the left is chairman Edwin Slinger. Less than three months later, McCreadie was sold to Luton Town for £5,500. It was another playing loss that Stanley could have done without, especially as McCreadie looked to have struck up an exciting partnership with Jackie Swindells, a striker who had been recently recruited from neighbours Blackburn Rovers.

Accrington v. Mansfield, FA Cup first round, 14 November 1959. Lawson Bennett challenges the Mansfield keeper with Terry Tighe (*left*) and Vincent Jack (*centre*) in close attendance. Stanley had reached the last thirty-two in the previous season and badly needed the revenue that a comparable run would have brought. However, Mansfield came away with a 2-1 victory, and this early FA Cup exit probably necessitated the sale of McCreadie. Ultimately, Harold Bodle proved not to be the answer to Accrington Stanley's managerial problems. After only four wins at Peel Park all season and with Stanley condemned to the Fourth Division, Bodle resigned in April 1960, just ten days from the end of the season. It was a sad end to his association with Accrington Stanley, for Bodle had been a fine servant and an inspirational captain during his playing days at Peel Park. In a feature in the *Accrington Observer* many years later, Bill Palmer wrote: 'For two seasons Bodle's commanding leadership from left-half – compounded of ruthless tackling and a cool old head – inspired and guided his side through many a tough spot. Harold could take a game by the scruff of the neck. He still has a wallet, presented to all twenty-two players, to mark the first of the highly popular floodlit matches against Scottish clubs. It was inscribed: "Accrington Stanley official souvenir for match bonus. May it never be empty." '

Unfortunately, empty was the only word that could describe Peel Park on 30 March 1960, when just 925 people turned out to watch Stanley take on York City, one of the smallest ever attendances for a League game at Peel Park. The faithful few were rewarded with a stirring 4-0 victory, Stanley's best result of the season. But the shockingly low gate was an all too clear sign that very tough times lay ahead for Accrington Stanley.

SOCCER STAR, March 25, 1961.   VOL. 9. NO. 27.   ONE SHILLING

★ **Two teams on the cover every week**

SOCCER STAR

ACCRINGTON 1961   Left to right (back): Smith, Tighe (now Crewe), Forrester, McInnes, Swindells, Sneddon. Left to right (front): Hudson, Logue, Harrower, Bennett, Devine.

Despite relegation to the Fourth Division, Stanley were still very much part of the Football League firmament, as this front cover of *Soccer Star* demonstrates. The photograph is the official Stanley first team at the start of the 1960/61 season, with Jimmy Harrower in a player-manager role. From left to right, back row: Smith, Tighe, Forrester, McInnes, Swindells, Sneddon. Front row: Hudson, Logue, Harrower, Bennett, Devine.

Above: Accrington Stanley's reserve team line-up at the start of the 1960/61 season. From left to right, back row: Graham Lord, Mike Ferguson, Gordon Stones, John Marshall, unknown, Ronnie Nightingale. Front row: unknown, Derek Sturrock, Bobby Gordon, Alex Hamilton, John Egan. Although in the reserve team line-up here, Alex Hamilton was a first team regular and one of the few surviving Galbraith signings at the club. Mike Ferguson was a son of Burnley who had left home to seek his playing fortunes with Plymouth Argyle. On leave in the summer of 1960, he approached Accrington Stanley, who signed him immediately. *Below:* Early season action at Peel Park as Stanley face Gillingham, on 12 September 1960. George Hudson, seen here challenging the Gills' 'keeper, hit a brilliant hat-trick in a 3-0 win.

Above: Action from Accrington's League encounter with Barrow, 26 September 1960. The Stanley player sending a header goalwards is George Hudson, who ended the 1960/61 season with 35 goals from 44 games, a remarkable achievement given that Stanley finished in a disappointing eighteenth position. *Below:* Another Hudson header in Stanley's 4-1 thrashing of Stockport County, 12 November 1960. From left to right, the other Stanley players are Jackie Swindells, Alex Hamilton and Mike Ferguson. That Accrington had such quality strikers as Swindells and Hudson was due to the generosity of Blackburn Rovers, who sold Swindells for just over £1,000 and let Hudson go for free.

Mike Ferguson in action. The Burnley Road stand, seen here in all its glory, was by now proving to be a real burden on Stanley's finances, increasingly fragile due to falling attendances and rapidly increasing costs.

In the 1960/61 FA Cup, Stanley fought past Barrow and Mansfield into the third round, where they drew First Division Preston at Deepdale. Here, Willie Devine and team-mates look to be in good spirits as they prepare for the game. The tie turned into one of Stanley's finest FA Cup occasions, as they secured a brilliant 1-1 draw in front of 20,268 spectators. Were it not for an inspired save by Preston 'keeper Else in the final minute to deny Jackie Swindells, Stanley would have pulled off a major cup upset. No wonder Stanley fans quietly fancied their chances in the replay.

Above: Bee captures both the humour and the gravity of the Preston replay, with financial considerations never far from mind. Unfortunately, God wasn't on Stanley's side in the replay as torrential rain ruined the game as a spectacle, with Preston running out easy 4-0 winners. *Left:* With Stanley out of the FA Cup, the Peel Park faithful had a long winter of Fourth Division football to look forward to. The replay against Preston had seen a 14,596 crowd descend on Peel Park, but the next League match attracted just 2,763, a disappointment to the club's leaders who hoped that the inspirational display at Preston would bring more support on a regular basis. Despite the gloominess of Bee, Stanley battled to eighteenth position and so avoided re-election.

Stanley line-up for the 1961/62 season. From left to right, back row: A. Hamilton, W. Smith. (player-coach), G. Richardson, M. Pickup, J. Walton. Middle row: C. Kilby (director), J. Harrower (manager), G. Forrester, A. Smith, P. Vipham, R. Wilson, J. Wigglesworth (secretary), R. Walton (director), E. Slinger (chairman). Front row: R. Gordon, L. Bennett, P. Irving, M. Ferguson, D. Sturrock, G. Hudson, P. Mulvey, W. Devine. Some familiar names are missing, the result of a controversial end-of-season clearout at Peel Park that saw goalkeeper Bill McInnes, Charlie Sneddon and Gordon Stones given free transfers. The listing of McInnes and Stones was especially divisive and was reportedly opposed by some members of the board. Stones was only twenty-six and had reputedly been the subject of past enquiries from First Division clubs. McInnes was an experienced 'keeper whose end-of-season form had kept Stanley out of the re-election places. Forward Jackie Swindells is also missing. He had suffered something of a loss of form during the latter stages of the season, but he still finished with a respectable 20 League and cup goals. Nonetheless, he was sold to Barnsley for a mere £750. Stanley's young full-back Graham Lord is another absentee from the squad. He had suffered a badly broken leg in a game against Bradford Park Avenue on Christmas Eve 1960 at a time when he was enjoying a successful run in the first team. He recovered to play once more, but never made the Stanley first team again. Lord's fate was an example of the misfortune that Stanley could ill afford. Manager Jimmy Harrower's summer was spent trying to put together a reasonable squad with virtually no resources, and he pulled off something of a masterstroke with the free signing of veteran full-back Joe Walton from Preston. This was followed by another defensive acquisition, also from Deepdale, in the shape of Garbutt Richardson. A clutch of other free signings completed Harrower's reconstruction of the team, and if he could have kept this squad together, Stanley would have had a decent chance of survival.

Stanley face Carlisle United at Peel Park on 9 September 1961. George Hudson, seen challenging fiercely for the ball, was again the man Stanley relied on to score goals, and he bagged the winner in this game as Stanley defeated the Cumbrians 1-0. The following week, a rare Alex Hamilton goal gave Stanley the points at Bradford City. With eight points from eight games, Accrington held a mid-table position and looked to be doing reasonably well. Disaster struck the following week, however, when Garbutt Richardson was badly injured at Barrow. Worse was to follow a fortnight later when Harrower was forced to sell George Hudson to Peterborough. The loss of Hudson and Richardson was a double blow from which Stanley would not recover. With Hudson gone, the teeth had been removed from Stanley's attack, and they scored just eight more goals in League football.

Other incidents served to undermine the confidence of the club. When Workington Town turned up for a League game in November 1961 and ran out in their usual away strip of white, it transpired that no-one from Accrington had told the Cumbrian club that Stanley themselves had changed their main strip from red shirts to white with a red band. In the end, Accrington played in white and Workington in Accrington's traditional colours of red. All those with Accrington Stanley at heart couldn't help but think that such incidents were indicative of a serious malaise within the very fabric of the club.

Accrington Stanley *v*. Bradford City, 3 February, 1962. Stanley lost this game 0-2 in front of just 1,554 spectators, their fifth consecutive game without scoring and their twelfth without victory. Whatever morale still existed at the club had been even further undermined by a bitter row that had broken out in the pages of the *Accrington Observer* following Stanley's FA Cup defeat at Hartlepool in November. It emerged that although 200 Stanley supporters had made the trek to the north east, neither the chairman, Edwin Slinger, nor any of the directors had bothered. Slinger told the paper that they had all had other commitments, but this did not wash with the players, supporters or with the *Accrington Observer* itself. The paper commented that: 'The club is now fighting for its very existence, and a strong lead is needed from the top down.' A letter from one of the fans who had gone to Hartlepool was less diplomatic: 'Now that Stanley are out of the Cup, who is going to give a lead to lift the club from the canvas before the count is taken? The weeks and months have passed by while paralysis has crept on and, as far as the public know, nothing but a disastrous inertia in the boardroom at Peel Park.'

In December 1961, the Supporters' Club, who had been keeping the club going with weekly donations of £300, convened a crisis meeting at Accrington Town Hall. The purpose of the meeting was to find new fund-raising initiatives to raise money towards the purchase of new players, this despite the club owing £3,000 in unpaid transfer fees. However, the meeting was wholly acrimonious, with the board of directors the main target for the supporters' vituperation. One supporter, Tom Langton, appealed for unity and suggested a combined operation that included the board, the Supporters' Club, the *Accrington Observer* and several of the town's dignitaries, including ex-chairman George Pratt. Mr Langton's suggestion was carried, but the evening ended on a sour note when the meeting voted not to take a collection. Dick Briggs, a leading member of the Supporters' Club who had made his way to the exit with a collecting box, was forced to retake his seat, muttering, 'Then God help football in Accrington.'

Stanley v. Rochdale, 24 February 1962. Front page appeals in the local press for the Accrington public to support their team preceded this League encounter, which proved to be Stanley's last ever at Peel Park, a 0-2 defeat at the hands of Rochdale. The crowd of 2,700 was an improvement on previous home attendances, but just a few miles down the road at Ewood Park, 33,194 turned out for a Blackburn-Burnley derby. Stanley's final two League games were away from home at Doncaster and Crewe. Stanley's penultimate game at Belle Vue attracted less than 2,000 spectators, clear evidence that they were not the only Fourth Division club struggling to survive on meagre gates.

By this time, Stanley had become a national news story. The escalation of Stanley's troubles was in part due to the Football League, who had involved themselves by writing to Stanley asking for clarification of their financial position, placing a temporary embargo on Stanley's transfer activities in the process. Sam Pilkington, the club's vice-president, had been asked to return to the boardroom to help the club through the immediate crisis. Pilkington agreed to the request, and he immediately contacted Alan Hardaker at the Football League to reassure him of Stanley's position. The crisis appeared to abate, but Pilkington reignited speculation by inviting Bob Lord, chairman of Burnley, to help out. Lord was a good friend of Pilkington, but many others at Stanley were deeply suspicious of him, particularly when he named his price of involvement as being the resignation of six directors.

Sam Pilkington is interviewed on television. Stanley's fate turned on a meeting of the club's creditors on 5 March, a Monday evening. The meeting listened to a plethora of debts, revealing the extent of the club's insolvency. Some liabilities, such as bank overdrafts and outstanding transfer fees, were commonplace in lower league football and were of little concern. But other debts were far more serious, particularly the £458 owing on the players' national insurance stamps. Neglecting to pay insurance stamps was an illegal practice more associated with corrupt tradesmen. Not one player had an insurance stamp on his card from June 1961 onwards. On hearing this, Pilkington withdrew his offer of assistance and Lord recommended that the club should cease activities.

The following day, 6 March, the club's remaining four directors met to decide what action to take in the light of the creditors' meeting. On the plus side, only a few creditors were demanding immediate payment. Of the £43,566 owed by Stanley, around £4,000 was needed in the short term to keep the club going. However, the directors clearly felt the situation was hopeless. They were unable to meet final demand notices for their supply of electricity, water and gas, without which the staging of League football would be impossible. The directors sent a letter of resignation to the League that very day.

When the players turned up for training, they were told the news by secretary Jack Wigglesworth. As they milled around and the club's property was brought out to be seized, a photo opportunity of rare poignancy was captured and relayed around the world. The public uproar that greeted the news of the club's resignation seems to indicate that the seriousness of Stanley's plight had not been appreciated. A couple of days later a man walked into Peel Park and put a bag on a table and said: 'You can borrow that interest free, and pay it back whenever you can manage it. I don't want to see this club go under.' In the bag was £10,000 in cash.

Paddy Mulvey (right), with Stanley washing lady Sally Dewhurst, seems to be enjoying the attention. Given such significant pledges of cash, William Cocker, Stanley's president, attempted to rescind the club's resignation. He told the press: 'The promises of money coming in are simply fantastic.' Stanley's survival rested with the secretary of the Football League, Alan Hardaker. It was in his remit to call an Emergency General Meeting at which Stanley could have been reprieved by a vote of her fellow clubs. Instead, Hardaker put the matter to the League Management Committee (member: Bob Lord) who chose to accept Stanley's original letter of resignation.

The resignation of Accrington Stanley from the Football League was accompanied by nostalgic eulogies in the national press but bitter accusations in the town. This photograph, taken at that last home game against Rochdale, illustrates what the essential problem was. The early 1960s saw a revival in the fortunes of Blackburn and Burnley. The Turf Moor club brought European Cup football to East Lancashire in 1961 and both reached FA Cup finals in 1960 and 1962 respectively. With two visits a season to East Lancashire of all the big First Division names, added of course to the Lancashire derbies, the Accrington public, perhaps understandably, chose to forsake the more humble offerings at Peel Park. This was the fatal consequence of Accrington's geography, the price of their ticket.

Another factor was the periodic appeal for money and support that Stanley undertook in the local press. On each of these occasions, the response was limited and temporary, but always enough to see the club through its immediate problems. There was little reason for the Accrington public to think any different of the 1962 crisis until it was too late. The players had also had enough of the uncertainties involved with a constant struggle for survival. There was resentment towards the board that no directors had turned up at the ground to let the players know officially that it was all over. George Forrester told the *Daily Mail*: 'As far as I am concerned the closedown is a good thing. We know at last where we stand. The writing was on the wall for Stanley when the few spectators who turned up at home matches began to jeer.' Willie Devine echoed this sentiment, telling the *Daily Herald*: 'It is sad to see the club die, but many of us are happy. It was time the club was wrapped up. Things had reached the stage where we were happier playing away from home.'

The last remaining formalities served merely to heighten the sense of injustice felt by those who had tried to save the club. The sight of creditors swooping on Peel Park to recoup their money was horrible, with even the playing kits being fished out of the washing tub to be set against debts. Mike Ferguson was sold for £2,000, and he later commanded a £60,000 fee when Blackburn sold him to Aston Villa. Goalkeeper Alex Smith, whose value was estimated at £10,000 at the start of the 1961/62 season, was sold for just £750. No wonder Stanley director Stan Armitage compared the creditors to vultures picking at the remains of a dead body.

The fans who had stuck with Stanley to the end had to come to terms with the sudden loss of their club. Ellen Rishton told the press: 'I can't understand anybody who isn't loyal to their home town team. I've often been despairing and sometimes I say I won't go to watch them, but I live near the ground and when I hear that first small cheer I get my coat on. I just don't know what I'll do now. It's like a death.'

The final twist of the knife came just one week after the club was wound up when Bradford Park Avenue sold Ian Gibson (*above*) to Middlesbrough. Gibson was a midfield prodigy, signed by Galbraith in 1958 and in Stanley's first team before his sixteenth birthday. He had been poached by Bradford in July 1959 aged just sixteen, before he could sign as a full-time professional and become subject to a transfer fee. His sale to Middlesbrough realised £20,000, a fee that Stanley thought should have been theirs and which would have saved the club from extinction.

78

Six

The Acorn Never Falls
Far From The Oak
1962-1970

In the post mortem that followed the resignation of Accrington Stanley from the League, it was the decision to acquire the Burnley Road stand that was seen to be the root of Stanley's fall, and those people responsible for that decision were the subject of some criticism. It is, of course, somewhat easier to criticise after the event. As Stanley challenged for the Third Division (North) title under Walter Galbraith, there was little argument that the ground needed to be developed. Peel Park's only stand had its foundations in the 1921 era, and even in the 1950s the entire seating capacity was just 800. Just as people became used to the standards of modern housing in the post-war era, football fans were no longer happy standing on dusty, shifting cinders. At the very least, a club had to provide concrete terracing and a cover to protect the public from the elements.

It was in this context, added to reasonably healthy crowds, that Stanley began to plan for a main stand on the Burnley Road side of the ground. Initial plans were put before the public in December 1953, and the club intended to create a separate company to raise the required £30,000 capital in shares. This plan never got underway, but the club always kept in mind the need to raise the seating capacity of the ground. By the late 1950s, the cost of a new construction had risen to over £40,000, clearly beyond Stanley's budget. From this perspective, the purchase and reconstruction of a huge 4,700-seat grandstand for around £15,000 in April 1958 represented an opportunity to significantly develop the ground with a minimal impact on finances.

In principle then, the decision to buy the stand was sound and was, incidentally, commended wholeheartedly by the local press who saw it as further evidence that Stanley were ahead of the game. If all had gone smoothly from this point on, then the stand would never have gained the infamy that it did. Unfortunately, events turned out rather differently. The cost of rebuilding the stand, the discovery that there was insufficient room to rebuild the full edifice, and the restricted views for those at the rear of the stand are well known and betray the hurried nature of the original purchase. But the real damage was done in the following two years when both the team and the crowds declined substantially. Had Accrington made it into the Second Division, with the increased gates that such a promotion would have entailed, the stand may have been worth the investment. As it was, Walter Galbraith's comment to a supporter proved to be sadly accurate: 'We'll never fill it, and I could have had three new players with the money.'

ALAS, POOR ACCRINGTON!

by John Macadam

A man and his dog—and the end of Accrington Stanley as a Football League club. Cold, desolate, empty, heartbreaking, for this groundsman and everyone else.

Typical of the media reaction to Stanley's demise was this headline from Charles Buchan's *Football Monthly*. A recurring theme was the belief that Stanley would prove to be just the first of many lower league clubs who would regretfully but unavoidably go out of business due to inexorable financial pressures. Other clubs mentioned in the article were Gillingham and Stockport. The article concluded that Accrington Stanley and their ilk were: '... the heavy brake on the natural progress which will take the Football League into a realist world in which football will be a truly global competition.'

Accrington Stanley, 1964. From left to right, back row: Bill Patterson (trainer), Ian Proctor, Don Bramley, Terry Neville, Charlie Wade, Ken Heywood, Ronnie Kershaw. Front row: Ray Pearson, Jackie Boyes, Peter Dunn, Jimmy Hinksman, Alan Leighton. Despite the end of League football in Accrington, Stanley continued to play until 1966 as an amateur club in the Lancashire Combination. To the immense credit of those involved and in the face of everything that had happened, football continued on a regular basis at Peel Park.

IN THE HIGH COURT OF JUSTICE   No. 001354 of 1963

CHANCERY DIVISION

COMPANIES COURT

IN THE MATTER OF ACCRINGTON STANLEY FOOTBALL COMPANY (1921) LIMITED

and

IN THE MATTER OF THE COMPANIES ACT, 1948

SUMMARY OF THE STATEMENT OF AFFAIRS

As at 2nd December, 1963 the date of the winding-up order.
Submitted by Stanley Armitage and George Clarkson, directors, on 22nd January, 1964.

Gross liabilities £		£	£	Estimated Realisable Values £
	ASSETS			
	NOT SPECIFICALLY PLEDGED			
	Balance at bank			3
	Book debt (arrears of rent receivable)			595
	Furniture, fittings, utensils, etc.			110
				708
	SPECIFICALLY PLEDGED		£	
8,440	Freehold land and buildings together with fixed plant and machinery		8,440	
	DEDUCT			
	Due to fully secured debenture holders (50)		8,440	
	Estimated total assets subject to costs of liquidation			708
	LIABILITIES			
305	Preferential creditors (3) for PAYE and other income tax, rates and National Insurance contributions			305
	Estimated balance of assets available for unsecured creditors			403
	Unsecured creditors (97) viz:-	£	£	
	Trade accounts		266	
	Outstanding expenses		8,779	
	Materials and work done		3,511	
	Income tax (PAYE and Schedule "D")		3,601	
	Bank overdraft		8,315	
	Loans – by present directors	4,428		
49,501	– by others	20,601	25,029	49,501
£58,246	Estimated deficiency as regards unsecured creditors			49,098
	CAPITAL ISSUED AND PAID UP, viz:-		£	
	14,498 ordinary shares of £1 each (3,162 shareholders)		14,498	
	Add:- Amount paid on 159 shares forfeited		61	
	Share capital subscription fund account		31	14,590
	Estimated total deficiency			£63,688

82

On 2 December 1963, a sad chapter in the history of Accrington football was played out in the Chancery Division of the High Court of Justice. A winding-up petition (*left*) was presented against Stanley, whose debts were estimated at £63,688. In order to avoid liability for these debts, Stanley were forced to drop their famous moniker, and this applied to the few remaining ground signs. A symbolic moment (*above*) as 'Stanley' is whitewashed from the walls of Peel Park.

If Peel Park was no longer the venue for professional football stars, it still occasionally hosted celebrities of a different kind. Here, Joe Brady, better known as Jock Weir in *Z-Cars*, signs autographs after an All Star XI had met a Burnley XI in May 1963.

The new, all-amateur Accrington Stanley found almost immediate success, winning the Lancashire Combination Second Division title in 1964. *Above:* Captain Jimmy Hinksman raises the trophy at Peel Park. An encouraging crowd of nearly 1,000 had turned out for Stanley's opening Lancashire Combination fixture, and though this declined through the winter months, the club found they could rely on the patronage of a few hundred fans. *Below:* Don Bramley displays his Lancashire Combination winners' shield. Along with Hinksman, Bramley would go on to be an integral part of the new Accrington Stanley, managing both the reserves and the first team.

Accrington Stanley *v.* Glossop, 8 January 1966. Stanley's victorious campaign of 1963/64 saw the club return to the Lancashire Combination First Division, the competition they had left in 1921 to enter the Football League. However, this was a strong league which contained many of the clubs who would, in just a few years' time, leave the Combination and play in the new Northern Premier League. Stanley were unable to compete financially, and the promotion-winning side of 1964 gradually broke up as the club suffered an immediate relegation.

The 1965/66 season was disastrous, and by the turn of the year Stanley propped up the table without a win in sixteen games. The club still played at Peel Park, but the ground had been bought by a scrap metal dealer who charged the club £7 per week rent. This took the weekly cost of running the club to around £30, but by the time of their resignation only £56 had been taken through the gate during the entire season. A search for a new ground proved fruitless, and so for the second time in four years, an Accrington town team called it a day and resigned from a league competition midway through the season. The media was notified that the fixture at home to Glossop would be Accrington Stanley's last at Peel Park, and once more the journalists turned up to write misty-eyed eulogies. The team rallied to end on a high note, defeating their opponents 3-2. But the scene is undeniably depressing – an old League ground hosting amateur football with little more than fifty people present.

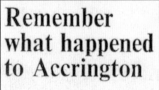

Remember what happened to Accrington

(DON'T LET THE GRASS GROW AT YOUR CLUB)

Above: Perhaps the most enduring image of Stanley's demise – a Football League commemorative shield planted gravestone-like against a backdrop of crumbling terraces and faceless hoardings. In the top right of the photo are the remains of the billboard for Whitewell Milk, and the circle that used to house the famous clock can still be seen. In November 1965, Stanley had asked the local council to buy Peel Park in an attempt to lay more solid financial foundations, but the council had refused. In the same week, Stockport Corporation bought Edgeley Park and rented it back to Stockport County for a nominal sum, saving the club from financial extinction in the process.

Left: The worst aspect of Stanley's demise was the fact that the ground was left to slowly decay. Peel Park was once at the heart of the town's being, as important in its way as the market and the Town Hall. This once-thriving place should not have been left to crumble before the eyes of the townsfolk. In its ruined state, Peel Park became an irresistible backdrop for more than the odd article in the football press, this example being from the *Football League Review*.

Peel Park, January 1969. Three senior Stanleyites remember the days of Mortimer and Mee. From left to right: Roger Eastwood, Absalom Parkinson and George Taylor, who had all watched the club for more than fifty years. At the time this photograph was taken, plans were underway for Accrington Stanley to represent the town once more.

Too young to remember even the last days of Stanley, some boys from the neighbouring Peel Park school play in the shadows of the old stand. Lancashire County Council finally bought Peel Park and spent £25,000 landscaping the ground. However, it took a fire to demolish the old stand, and not before an eleven-year-old girl had sustained two broken legs falling from the roof as she played with friends.

Councillor Bill Parkinson was one of the main figures behind the resurrection of Accrington Stanley in the late 1960s. In the first week of July 1968, the *Accrington Observer* ran an article in which Bill articulated his belief that Accrington should seek to re-establish a town team. The reaction to the councillor's proposition was enthusiastic, and a series of public meetings culminated in a fund-raising friendly in August 1968 in which an Accrington revival team played local rivals Great Harwood, then in the Northern Premier League. It was hoped that the Accrington public would support the team in numbers, but in the event only around fifty turned up to see a makeshift Accrington side hammered 9-0 by strong opposition. It was a lesson in the learning that the re-establishment of a team would have to be a slow and organic process.

Undeterred by the Harwood game, a new club – Accrington Stanley 1968 – was officially formed with the goal of entering Stanley into the Lancashire Combination for the start of 1969/70. But there was a veritable mountain to climb before a ball could be kicked. In October 1968, *Accrington Observer* journalist David Allen reported that the minimum annual running costs of a struggling Second Division Combination team was £1,500, and this rose to £4,000 for a good First Division set up. With just £130 in the bank, Stanley had to set their sights on a distant target.

In May 1969, Stanley committee member Jack Barrett set off on a sponsored walk to Liverpool to raise funds for the new club. The Mayor gave Jack a civic send off, and his efforts raised £100. By the time of this fundraising effort, interest in the new Stanley was growing. The club had not met their initial target of competing in the 1969/70 season, but the acquisition of a new ground in November 1969 finally convinced many interested onlookers that Accrington Stanley were once again in business. Stanley's new home was behind a public house called the Crown Inn, and became known as the Crown Ground. Whilst fundraising continued apace, the club announced that they would definitely be competing in 1970/71.

In May 1970, Jimmy Hinksman was named as the manager of the new Accrington Stanley. He had the daunting task of constructing a new team from nothing, but an interesting side-effect of the demise of the old Stanley had been the emergence of the Accrington and District Combination as one of the strongest amateur leagues in Lancashire. By the time Hinksman came to put together his team, the Accrington Combination numbered seventy clubs who attracted some 3,000 spectators between them on a Saturday afternoon. The new manager expressed his hope that some good recruits would emerge from the ranks of the local amateur league.

That Stanley were starting again from nothing is emphasised by this photograph of the construction of a new pavilion at the Crown Ground, taken in April 1970. From left to right: Harry Stevenson, Tom McColm, George Butler, Stephen Barrett, Charlie Tuck, Bill Parkinson, Alf Band and John Duckworth. In June 1970, the club was elected to the Lancashire Combination, the opening day of the season being set for 15 August. After two years of determined fundraising, the club had less than two months to complete the ground and build a team. Work continued on the ground, and in the face of some media qualms about a lack of signings, the Accrington Stanley team slowly began to take shape. Terry Tighe, who had made 117 League appearances for Stanley between 1957 and 1960, joined as player-coach, and a number of Accrington Combination players were signed for the reserve team. On 8 August, Stanley unveiled their part-time professionals: Stuart Illingworth, Mel Widdup and Benny Newell, all respected players signed from other local clubs. A friendly against Great Harwood resulted in a narrow 1-2 defeat for Stanley, an encouraging sign that they would be able to compete in the Lancashire Combination. On the eve of Stanley's return, that small band of enthusiasts could reflect on a satisfactory outcome to what had been a speculative venture. The *Accrington Observer*, ever willing to promote the cause, wrote: 'The *Observer* congratulates these civic-minded football enthusiasts who for two years have doggedly worked towards their goal while others sneered and jeered. Nothing has happened in the past two years to indicate that Accrington wants a football team. The public has not warmed to the idea: local businessmen have coolly ignored all appeals for help. But they hid their disappointment well.'

Bill Parkinson had indeed nurtured the process with a considered display of optimism and tact. He was careful not to let the process get ahead of itself, only ever sounding hopeful to the local press, but always encouraging those around him that the goal would be attained. Thus it was that Accrington – literally, the town where acorns grow – planted a tiny green seed of footballing hope.

Seven

Back in Business
1970-1986

Jimmy Hinksman introduces the Mayor of Accrington, Alan Benson, to the players before Accrington Stanley's opening Lancashire Combination fixture against Formby Town at the Crown Ground, 15 August 1970. The four players nearest to the camera are, from left to right: Jim Howley, John Nuttall, Braithwaite and Alan Davies.

Stanley *v*. Formby Town: Accrington fans celebrate as Alan Davies puts Stanley 2-1 ahead late into the second half. Stanley played out the remainder of the game to record a famous victory in front of hundreds of fans. It was an occasion for everyone in the town to be proud of and a vindication for those who had worked tirelessly behind the scenes to re-establish the club.

A view of the Crown Ground, 1971. As well as building drains under the pitch and enclosing the ground, the people behind the new Stanley had built a pavilion and changing rooms. Altogether, it had been a significant burden for just a few people to shoulder. Stanley's first season back was entirely satisfactory, as the team completed their fixtures to finish in sixth position. During the summer of 1971, manager Hinksman moved to strengthen the squad in order that Stanley could challenge for honours. A key signing was striker Colin Smith and with the squad strengthened in other areas, Stanley went into the 1971/72 season looking for some silverware to underline their return.

A triumphant end to the 1971/72 season, as captain Mel Widdup lifts the Lancashire Combination Cup. The player on the far left of the shot is Stuart Illingworth, whose 32 goals that season also helped to lift Stanley to runners-up position in the Lancashire Combination. Although on the face of it a fine season, a poor start and low gates had led to worrying headlines in the local press questioning the future of the club. A superb collective spirit had seen the team through, but it was a reminder to all concerned that the club was delicately balanced on a financial tightrope.

Accrington Stanley, May 1972. Players and coaching staff only, from left to right, back row: Jimmy Hinksman (manager), Mel Widdup, Dave Baron, Dick Ellis, Peter Dunn (trainer). Middle row: Benny Newell, Kenny Miller, Tony Farrell, Jim Howley, Stuart Illingworth. Front row: Ian Wilcox, David Hinksman, Alan Davies, Colin Smith.

Stanley made a return to Peel Park on 4 March 1973, when problems with drainage made the Crown Ground surface unplayable. It was hoped that the chance to see Accrington Stanley once more take the field at their famous old ground would tempt many more people to the match, but it poured with rain throughout. This, added to the fact that Peel Park no longer had any covered accommodation, dampened the occasion in more ways than one, but over 700 people endured the conditions, and some had even made a special effort to welcome their heroes home. In the game itself, Stanley drew 2-2 with Nelson.

Accrington Stanley, May 1973. Players only, middle row: Keith Windle, Andy Breckell, Jim Howley, Benny Newell. Front row: Mel Widdup, Tony Farrell, Stuart Illingworth, Alan Davies, Graham Bisby, Tommy Beard, Don Bramley, Dave Baron, David Hinksman. This team retained the Combination Cup, and formed the core of the all-conquering 1973/74 side. With the important addition of players like Ian McCrae, John Hubberstey and Dave McDowell, Stanley enjoyed a superb 1973/74 campaign that culminated in a Lancashire Combination League and Cup double.

Many Stanley fans wondered how good Jimmy Hinksman's side really was, and in November 1974 they had the chance to see Stanley compete against Altrincham, one of the best non-League outfits in the country, in an FA Cup fourth qualifying round tie. Although Stanley lost 0-3, the game had been evenly balanced before John Hubberstey was taken out of the game by an Altrincham elbow. It had been Stanley's best FA Cup run since their reformation, and their opponents progressed to the fourth round where they were eventually beaten by Everton.

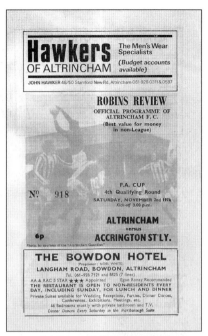

In May 1975, Stanley organised a testimonial for the manager and players who had been instrumental in the success of the club. From left to right: Mel Widdup, Dave Baron, Stuart Illingworth, Benny Newell and Jimmy Hinskman. However, by this time Hinksman was Stanley's ex-manager. Having won all of the Lancashire Combination's major honours, the next step for Stanley was to move to a higher grade of football, but the appalling state of the Crown Ground pitch negated such a move, and the Council baulked at the £7,500 cost of a proper drainage system. Hinksman resigned in April when he was told that additional wage money would not be made available for the following season. Frustration at Stanley's inability to move up in the non-League world with what was clearly a highly talented side also contributed to Hinksman's decision.

Above: New Stanley manager Don Bramley *(centre left)* and Bill Parkinson *(centre right)* with the agenda for the club's annual meeting, August 1975. On the back left of the photograph is John Alty, who was then Stanley treasurer and secretary, but who would go on to become one of the club's most high profile chairmen. To the right of Bill Parkinson is trainer Tony Clements, still an active figure at the Crown Ground today. At the meeting, it was revealed that fundraising had yielded £2,219, vital income that enabled the club to post a £116 profit.

Right: The 1975/76 season also saw a return for Stanley on the football pools coupon when their home fixture against Leyland Motors on April 21 was listed. Along with Nottingham Forest, Stanley were the only club with an unblemished home record, and they didn't let the punters down, defeating Leyland 5-1. At the end of the season, Blackburn Rovers approached Stanley, hoping to take Dave Hargreaves on loan. Stanley refused, telling their League neighbours that if they wanted the striker they would have to pay a fee for him.

Weekend forecasts

HOME FORM	'D'	LEAGUE—Division I	AWAY FORM		'A' Sel.
WDDDD	12	Aston Villa v. Middlesbrough	LWWLL	12-5	1
WLLWD	11	Everton v. West Ham	LDLLL	11-9	1
DLWDD	20	Leicester v. Man. Utd.	WDWWL	16-8	X
WWWWW	14	Man. City v. Arsenal	LWDLD	9-5	1
LDWWD	13	Tottenham v. Newcastle Utd.	LLDDL	13-11	1

		LEAGUE—Division II			
WWDDW	10	Bristol C. v. Notts County	DWLLD	9-6	1
DDLWD	11	Carlisle Utd. v. Plymouth	LDDDL	9-9	1
WDWDW	10	Charlton v. Bolton W.	DLDLD	15-8	1
WLWWD	20	Fulham v. Blackburn Rov.	DLWLL	9-10	X
WWWDD	11	Luton Tn. v. Blackpool	DLWDL	8-8	1
WWWWW	9	Nottm F. v. Bristol Rov.	LLWDL	6-11	1
DDDDW	11	Oldham Ath. v. West Brom.	LWWLD	10-9	2
LLWDD	21	Orient v. Oxford Utd.	LWLWL	10-10	X
LDWWW	4	Sunderland v. Portsmouth	LWLLL	5-9	1
LWWWW	15	York City v. Chelsea	DLWLD	3-9	1

		LEAGUE—Division III			
WDWWW	11	Brighton v. Sheff. Wed.	DLLLD	8-9	1
DLLWW	21	Halifax Tn. v. Aldershot	LLLLD	8-13	X
WLDWD	10	Hereford v. Rotherham	DDLDL	8-8	1
DWDDW	9	Mansfield v. Colchester	LLDLD	13-9	1
DLWDL	22	Peterborough v. Shrewsbury	DLDLL	14-5	X
LWWDW	11	Preston NE v. Port Vale	WDLDL	4-12	1
DLWWL	20	Swindon Tn. v. Walsall	LWDWD	7-11	X

		LEAGUE—Division IV			
WWDWD	12	Barnsley v. Southport	DDDLL	10-7	1
DDWLL	13	Bradford C. v. Cambridge	LDWLL	9-10	1
DWWWW	15	Darlington v. Bournemouth	LLLDD	5-8	1
LWWWL	14	Hartlepool v. Brentford	LLWLD	9-9	1
WLDDW	10	Huddersfield Tn. v. Watford	DWLWL	9-6	1
LLLDL	11	Newport v. Workington	LLLLW	8-4	1
LDWWD	9	Reading v. Crewe Alex.	WLDWL	7-8	1
WWDDW	22	Torquay Utd. v. Lincoln C.	LWWDW	8-5	X

Swansea v. Rochdale void on coupons

		SCOTTISH PREMIER			
LWLLD	18	Aberdeen v. Hibernian	WLLWD	7-10	2
WWWWD	10	Celtic v. Ayr Utd.	LLWWL	5-9	1
WWDWW	18	Dundee Utd. v. Rangers	WWWWD	6-6	2
WDLWL	5	Hearts v. St. Johnstone	LLDLL	10-4	1
DWWWW	8	Motherwell v. Dundee	LWLLD	10-9	1

		CHESHIRE COUNTY LEAGUE			
WWWWD	10	Chorley v. Stalybridge	LDWDL		1
LDDLW	18	Darwen v. Marine	WWWDL		2
WWDDW	20	Horwich v. Formby	LDDDL		X
LLDWL	17	New Mills v. Middlewich	LLLWD		2
WWLLW	19	Radcliffe v. New Brighton	WDWLW		2
WLWLL	20	Rhyl v. Hyde Utd.	LDLDW		X
DLLDW	18	Rossendale v. Leek	WWLLW		2
WDWWW	21	St. Helens v. Nantwich	WDWLW		X
DWWDD	13	Witton Alb. v. Droylsden	WLLWL		1

		LANCASHIRE COMBINATION			
WWWWW	11	Accrington v. Leyland M.	DWDWL		1
WDWWL	16	Atherton v. Bootle	LWDWW		2
DLWWW	18	Bacup v. Blackpool M.	LDWLL		2
LLDDW	10	Colne v. Ashton	LLLLL		X
WWDLL	21	Ford M. v. Clitheroe	DDLDD		1
WDDWW	20	Kirby v. Nelson	WWWWW		X
WDLWD	12	Lytham v. Wren	WLLDW		1
WWLLL	11	M'cambe Rs. v. Skelm'd'le Rs.	DDLLL		1

		NORTHERN LEAGUE			
DWDWD	11	Crook v. Ferryhill	LWDLL		1
WWDWL	12	Penrith v. Shildon	LDDDD		1

Left: Stanley line up before a 4-0 win over Ashton Town, 10 January 1976. From left to right, back row: T. Clements (trainer), Baron, Burr, Ellis, Wilcox, Hargreaves, Chapman, Bushell, D. Bramley (manager). Front row: Brydon, Davies, Parr, Shaw, McDowell.

This was a team of some considerable talent. Goalkeeper Dick Ellis had played for the England Youth team in 1970, and was one of the best non-League custodians in the county. Defender Glyn Burr was spotted by Bury whilst playing for Stanley and was invited for trials, whilst Jack Brydon was selected for the Lancashire FA representative team. Alan Davies also had Lancashire FA honours to his name. But the star of this side was undoubtedly striker Dave Hargreaves. Spotted by Don Bramley whilst playing Accrington Combination football, Hargreaves must rate as one of the most natural strikers Accrington Stanley have ever possessed. In 1975/76, he netted 56 goals in 43 league and cup appearances, whilst his partner Jack Brydon managed 35 from 42 games. Despite scoring 131 goals during the season, Stanley failed to win any honours.

Stanley with the Lancashire Combination Championship Trophy, May 1978. From left to right, back row: Dave Hindle, Ronnie Haworth, Bernie Poole, Ian Warburton, Keith Walkden, Jack Brydon. Middle row: Kevin Twinney, John Lamb, Gary Hilton, Alan Davies, Tony Clements (trainer). Front row: Ian McCrae, Mick McHugh, Ian Wilcox, Dave Parr. A couple of familiar faces were missing – manager Don Bramley and Dave Hargreaves. Bramley was sacked in January 1978, officially due to differences with the Board, but the manager himself expressed bemusement at the decision. His dismissal couldn't have been motivated by results. Stanley were at the top of the league and had once more underlined their potential with a pre-season defeat of Macclesfield Town. Reserve team manager Dave Baron stepped up to the first-team post. In February 1978, Dave Hargreaves finally made his move into professional football with Blackburn Rovers. The League club paid Stanley £1,000 after a two-month trial period had seen him play in two full League games for Rovers, though in unfortunate circumstances both times. His debut came on a bog of a pitch at Bloomfield Road, and his second appearance was on an equally hopeless frozen surface at Ewood Park. Both matches were televised and watched avidly by Stanley fans rooting for their hero. Blackburn didn't place much faith in the Stanley man, offering him a contract only until the end of the 1977/78 season. Bill Palmer of the *Accrington Observer* wasn't impressed: 'The Rovers' directors could have been more generous and given this young married man with a family the greater security of a contract covering next season, for what remains of this one is hardly long enough for him to prove that he is higher class material.'

The 1977/78 season marked the end of Accrington Stanley's involvement in the Lancashire Combination. The club had been searching for a new league which offered the hope of advancement, and it came in December 1977 with the announcement that the Cheshire League were forming a second tier. The secretary of the Lancashire Combination, Ken Dean, was desperate not to lose any more clubs to the Cheshire League, and sought to assure Stanley that their best interests lay in the Combination. In the preface to Stanley's 1977/78 yearbook, he wrote: 'We shall carry on, sparing no effort to ensure a bright future for Lancashire's premier county league. Mark my words, the Combination powers-that-be mean business. We are building a League fit for ambitious and go-ahead clubs who won't need to look elsewhere for a competitive and rewarding game of football.' Unfortunately for Dean, the Accrington board felt the case for moving to a higher standard of football was unanswerable, and Stanley's resignation ended an association with the Lancashire Combination that went back to 1901.

Dave Hargreaves in action for Blackburn Rovers *v.* Luton Town, 11 February 1978. Blackburn decided that two first-team games and a handful of reserve appearances were enough to judge the player, and he returned to Stanley in September 1978. Hargreaves would remain a Crown Ground favourite until February 1985, by which time he had scored an incredible 309 goals in 322 games.

NORTHERN PREMIER LEAGUE

LATICS REVIEW

Wigan Athletic

versus   versus

RUNCORN   **ACCRINGTON**
                     STANLEY

Northern Premier League   Lancs. Junior Cup — Semi-Final

Friday, 17th March K.O. 7-30 p.m.   Saturday, 18th March K.O. 3 p.m.

Official Programme   —   10p

Stanley's 1977/78 run in the Lancashire Junior Cup provided ample proof that the club ought to be competing at a higher level. In the quarter-finals, they defeated their Northern Premier League neighbours Great Harwood after a replay, and in the semi-final travelled to Wigan Athletic, who were just months from being elected to the Football League. Stanley held a 3-1 lead before finally going down 3-4 to a late Wigan onslaught, but it had been a fine performance against senior opposition.

Action from the Lancashire Junior Cup quarter-final against Great Harwood at the Showground, 25 February 1978. Harwood 'keeper John Wood claims the ball ahead of Stanley striker Jack Brydon. From left to right, other Stanley players in the frame are: Keith Walkden, Bernie Poole and Dave Parr. Stanley equalised in the last minute (1-1) and won the replay at the Crown Ground, 2-0.

Stanley take on Marine at the Crown Ground in a Lancashire Junior Cup tie, 5 January 1979. Marine were then the current Cheshire League champions and were the sort of team Stanley aspired to meet on a weekly basis. This was Stanley's first season in the Cheshire League, and were it not for an indifferent start they might have won promotion at the first attempt.

An Accrington Stanley matchday programme from the 1979/80 season. The inside front covers of this particular series were taken up by reflections on the old Stanley, and this programme (for a fixture against Skelmersdale United, on 1 December 1979) focused on the visit of Fulham to Peel Park in November 1955 as part of Stanley's series of floodlit friendlies. With a team that included Jimmy Hill and two future England managers in Ron Greenwood and Bobby Robson, Fulham were beaten 2-0 by a classy performance from one of Galbraith's great sides.

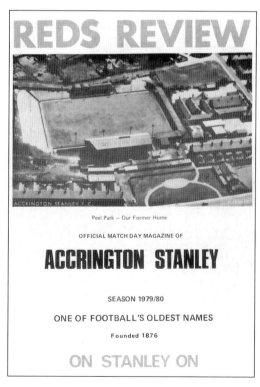

REDS REVIEW

Peel Park – Our Former Home

OFFICIAL MATCH DAY MAGAZINE OF

ACCRINGTON STANLEY

SEASON 1979/80

ONE OF FOOTBALL'S OLDEST NAMES

Founded 1876

ON STANLEY ON

Accrington Stanley, 1979/80. From left to right, back row: Frank Aspinall, Tony Clements, Kevin Twinney, Rob Haworth, Mick Finn, Dave Mooney, Ian Warburton, Keith Walkden, John Blackburn, Ian Berry. Front row: Simon Clark, Ian Wilcox, Dave Parr, Dave Hargreaves, David Eastwood. After a solid inaugural season in the Cheshire League, Stanley were one of the favourites for promotion as the 1979/80 season kicked off. Sure enough, with Dave Hargreaves in top goalscoring form, Stanley challenged for one of the top two promotion places throughout the season. But a problem loomed on the horizon. The pitch and surrounding facilities did not meet Cheshire League First Division standards. A visit in February 1980 from Cheshire League officials confirmed that if Stanley were to go up they had to upgrade the Crown Ground, and they gave the club a summer deadline. Although promotion had yet to be won, a small team of volunteers immediately started work on the required ground improvements.

In an extremely close finish to the season, Stanley secured the runners-up position on goal difference, but celebrations had to be put on hold until the Cheshire League gave their verdict on the ground. In June, the league officials visited the club and were shown the ground improvements. But despite the best efforts of the Stanley workers, the officials still thought the ground below the required standard. Director Mel Clay persuaded the League to give Stanley more time, during which the club carried out yet more improvements, but it was all in vain. At the annual meeting of the Cheshire League, Stanley were told that they would not be allowed to take their place in the First Division.

Stanley managed to force an FA tribunal to investigate the matter, and they were given the opportunity to present their case. However, Stanley were unable to convince the FA to reverse the Cheshire League's judgement. It was a bitter blow and something of a setback, but the reaction of the club was commendable. A new Supporters' Club was formed to galvanise the fund-raising and manpower efforts of the club towards ground development. By December 1980, a £10,000 upgrade of the Crown Ground was underway. This time, it seemed, nothing would be left to chance.

Above: Dave Hargreaves raises the Cheshire League Second Division championship trophy and Glyn Burr the Second Division Challenge Shield after Stanley had completed a divisional double, May 1981. Hargreaves was also awarded the league's Player of the Year accolade for the second successive season. *Below:* Stanley fans of all vintages celebrate the club's promotion to the Cheshire League First Division by taking to the streets on a carnival float! After enormous efforts that had seen the Crown Ground closed for the final part of the 1980/81 season and Stanley playing their home games on Darwen's Anchor Ground, the Cheshire League finally gave the Crown Ground a clean bill of health and confirmed Stanley's place in the Cheshire League First Division.

Accrington Stanley, 1981/82. From left to right, back row: D. Baron (manager), Burr, Moffatt, Mooney, Finn, Clark, Lamb, Adams, Cookson, T. Clements (trainer). Front row: Parr, Mason, Blackburn, Hargreaves, Twinney, Bolton. Their promotion to the Cheshire League First Division saw Stanley reach their first level in non-League football as they struggled to make their mark in the face of numerous on and off-field problems. The Crown Ground pitch continued to cause difficulties, and a spate of home postponements upon the commencement of the 1981/82 season sparked a cash flow crisis at the club. This turned into something of a public relations disaster when the Supporters' Club declared that it would pay the wages of the club's semi-professionals, only for the Board to belatedly turn down the offer. The problem was overcome, but not without the resignation of chairman John Prescott. John Alty returned to the club from a position at Stalybridge Celtic to assume the chairmanship. To add to the sense of upheaval, March 1982 saw Dave Baron resign as manager, ending four years in charge of first-team affairs. His replacement, goalkeeper Mick Finn, was only Stanley's fourth manager in twelve years, but Stanley were to find it difficult from this point in to establish a managerial team with any degree of longevity.

The next few years saw the club gradually consolidate their position in non-League football. A reorganisation in 1983 saw the Lancashire Combination and Cheshire Leagues come together to form the three-tiered North West Counties League, and Stanley were elected to the First Division. The team hit the headlines in October 1983 when they travelled to Gateshead in an FA Cup third qualifying round replay and came away with an excellent 2-1 win. This prompted a write-up in *The Guardian*, but this article also revealed that Stanley were a worrying £47,000 in debt, having been forced to spend £25,000 on the Crown Ground pitch.

It was also at this time that the rise of Clitheroe undermined Stanley's position as the senior non-League side in the area. Under the stewardship of Eric Whalley, Clitheroe won an unprecedented hat-trick of North West Counties League championships, culminating in a First Division title in 1985/86. Stanley themselves had finished mid-table, and the resignation of manager Frank O'Kane in May 1986 prompted Stanley to see if Eric Whalley could weave his magic at the Crown Ground. He was confirmed as Stanley manager in August 1986, and brought a number of his Clitheroe players with him. The 1986/87 season was the most eagerly awaited for many a year, and not just because of the arrival of a new and proven manager. That summer, the Football League confirmed that the top non-League team in the country would be promoted into the Football League, with a League club falling into the Football Conference. For many Stanley fans, it offered the first tantalising glimpse of a hitherto unreachable place. Accrington Stanley could see a road back to the Football League.

Eight

The Longest Road Will Take Us Home

1986-2001

John Coleman (left) and Jimmy Bell, the managerial team who in 1999/2000 brought Stanley their first championship since 1981, when they guided the team to the Unibond First Division title.

Accrington Stanley line-up for a pre-season friendly, July 1986. From left to right, back row: Chris Chisholm, Mick Robinson, Dave Mottershead, Dave Mooney, Steve Parry, Duncan Seddon, Dave Tattersall. Front row: Mick Ashcroft, Peter Rigby, Dave Sharples, Martin Eatough, Neil Rowbotham, Chris Grimshaw. Four of these players – Eatough, Sharples, Robinson and Ashcroft – had joined Eric Whalley in moving to the Crown Ground from Clitheroe. Striker Steve Parry was embarking on his fourth season at Stanley. Parry had been handed the task of replacing Dave Hargreaves as the team's main goalscorer, but he proved himself equal to the challenge, scoring over a century of goals for the club in 286 games. Right-back Neil Rowbotham was another loyal Stanley servant, who accumulated 276 appearances between 1981 and 1988.

Mick Robinson expertly executes a penalty in Stanley's 1-1 draw with Leek Town, 11 October 1986. The floodlights were a recent addition to the Crown Ground, having been bought from North London non-Leaguers Enfield. The lights were fairly rudimentary, but as well as illumination they also signalled Stanley's ambitions. For a club that claimed a return to League status as its avowed intention, the acquisition of floodlights was both a necessary and important step along that path.

As was the case at Peel Park, the addition of floodlights gave Stanley an additional dimension in terms of being able to stage Saturday games at 3 p.m. throughout the year, as well as evening kick-offs. For the first time, Stanley were able to compete in the Lancashire Floodlight League and the lights proved particularly useful for staging cup games. This action is from a Lancashire Cup replay *v.* Darwen, December 1986.

Captain Martin Eatough blasts a shot towards goal in blizzard conditions at the Crown Ground. Dave Tattersall is the Stanley player on the right. Eatough had been part of Clitheroe's all-conquering side and in this, his first season at Stanley, he led the club to the runners-up position behind Stalybridge Celtic. Promotion to the HFS Loans League First Division was a highly satisfactory conclusion to Eric Whalley's first season as manager.

Chris Grimshaw in his first spell at the Crown Ground. Along with fellow Stanley favourite Ashley Hoskin, Chris had been an apprentice at Burnley before being released without any real assessment by John Bond. He also spent time at Crewe and Bury before joining Stanley in July 1986. In three spells for the club, he made a record 362 appearances and scored 52 goals from midfield and defence. A hugely popular player on the terraces, his wholehearted approach to the game won him many lasting friends at Stanley.

Accrington Stanley, 1987/88. From left to right, back row: John Taylor, Mick Robinson, Pete Hutchinson, Mick Ashcroft, Andy Holden, Steve Parry, Steve O'Brien (trainer), Phil Leather (physiotherapist). Front row: Gary Butcher, Chris Grimshaw, Dave Sharples, Martin Eatough, Geoff Tyson, Neil Rowbotham, Neil Hanson. With largely the same squad, Stanley came within a whisker of a second successive promotion. Their final home game of the 1987/88 season attracted a crowd of 1,100, evidence that a winning team could draw substantial levels of support. Unfortunately, Stanley missed out, and the resignation of manager Eric Whalley shortly afterwards saw this team break up completely.

Colne Dynamoes *v.* Accrington Stanley, 21 October 1988. Stanley's commendable progress in the late 1980s was overshadowed by the startling rise of Colne Dynamoes. Stanley (in stripes) lost this encounter 0-5, but in the home game forced a 2-2 draw in front of 2,015 spectators. 1988/89 saw Colne win the HFS First Division title while Stanley finished sixth under the guidance of Gary Pierce, the former Wolves goalkeeper, in what was his first season as a manager. In what was bound to be a season of consolidation, the top six finish was entirely laudable.

Stanley signed Ian Britton for the 1989/90 season. Although he is perhaps best known in the football world for his long service at Chelsea, Britton also made a notable contribution to the story of East Lancashire football by scoring the goal that kept Burnley in the Football League, a header in the 2-1 victory over Orient in May 1987.

Stanley line up before the final fixture of the 1989/90 season. From left to right, back row: Tony Clements (physiotherapist), Alec Davies, Steve Guest, Martin White, Kenny Quigg, Jim Cameron, Graham Jones, Mark Walsh, Tibor Szabo, Gus Wilson, Andy Bondswell, Phil Leather (kit manager). Front row: Ian Britton, Chris Grimshaw, Paul Webb (assistant manager), Dave Thornley (manager), Dave Lutkevitch, Alan Crompton. Once more, Stanley had suffered an untimely managerial departure as Gary Pierce had resigned in October 1989 with Stanley going well in the league. It was thought that differences with the Board precipitated his leaving.

With Stanley going all out for promotion, it was decided that continuity was the best policy, and Pierce's assistant Dave Thornley was given the job. Although Stanley topped the table in December, a poor run of New Year form seemed to have foiled their promotion bid, but a storming run of six victories in March and April lifted the team back into contention. However, three defeats in the last three games frustrated Stanley's ambitions once again. That Stanley were investing in their squad is borne out by the presence of players like Andy Bondswell, a strong and very fast centre forward who cost the club £1,000, and Gus Wilson, who went on to have a distinguished career at Crewe Alexandra.

Accrington Stanley Under-18s with the Lancashire FA Under-18s Cup, May 1990. From left to right, back row: Roland Wilde (secretary), Don Bramley (coach), Andrew Proctor, Neil Gorton, Jamie Livesey, Frank Tunstall, Neil Dunleavy, Paul Fitzpatrick, Anthony Joyce, David Hinksman (manager), Alan Crane (physiotherapist). Front row: David Mason, Steve Czapowski, James Hodgson, Lee Bonnick, Andrew Thompson, Craig Dewhurst. The capture of the Lancashire FA County Cup was a significant achievement for Stanley in what was the club's first venture into youth teams. The initiative involved a couple of familiar faces – Don Bramley and David Hinksman – both ex-Stanley players. The under-18 team had the blessing of first-team manager Gary Pierce, but there were resource implications even though the entire project was run voluntarily. The axing of the youth set up due to costs in 1991 was a controversial decision regretted by most supporters, since it broke up a group of promising players committed to the club and ended the possibility of Stanley nurturing future first-team players.

Left: A group of Stanley veterans line up for a charity fixture at the Crown Ground. From left to right, back row: Tony Nuttall, John Nuttall, Jim Howley, Stuart Illingworth, Dave Baron, Benny Newell, Don Bramley, Jimmy Hinksman, Dick Ellis. Front row: Dave Hargreaves, Dave McDowell, Dave Parr, Tommy Beard, Ian McCrae, Ian Wilcox. Full-back Ian Wilcox gave exemplary service to Stanley, appearing over 300 times for the club between 1972 and 1980. He picked up two Lancashire Combination winners' medals and four Combination Cup winners' medals.

Stanley manager Phil Staley (front left) and the managing directors of Holland's Pies (middle) and Gibson's Sports (right) unveil a new Stanley shirt. Holland's Pies became Accrington Stanley club sponsors in July 1990, and their patronage was most welcome at a time when the club was still suffering from financial uncertainties. Phil Staley, a non-League manager with vast experience and unrivalled contacts, took over from Dave Thornley in November 1990. He began to build his own side, and his first signing was to be one of his most important. Stanley paid Rossendale United £1,000 for the services of striker Paul Beck. The players standing behind Phil Staley were a fine team that made a notable piece of club history in the FA Cup of 1992/93. From left to right: Mike Lutkevitch, Paul Burns, Bernie Hughes, Terry Williams, Paul Collings, Charlie Cooper, Eddie Johnson, Martin Clark, Stuart Owen, Paul Beck, Steve Lampkin.

Staley had guided Stanley to fourth position in the HFS Loans First Division in 1990/91, but the resignation from the Premier Division of South Liverpool left a vacancy in the top division. The side that had finished one place above Stanley in third was Worksop Town, but their ground was not up to standard and they could not upgrade it in time. Where once Stanley had suffered they now gained, as their promotion to the HFS Loans Premier Division was confirmed. However, as is so often the case in non-League football, a higher grade of football stretched the club to their financial limits. In July 1992, with a successful first Premier League season behind them, Stanley appealed in the local press for more support for their fundraising schemes. Chairman John Alty told the *Accrington Observer*: 'The present squad looks to be an extremely strong one. It is, however, essential that our income is increased substantially if we are to fund the payments to the quality players which we possess. If the supporters want Stanley to survive at this level, they must come forward and help.' The appeal attracted a good response, and the club gradually alleviated its most pressing debts. But if the fans played their part in the 1992/93 season, so did the team, who were to embark on a thrilling run in the FA Cup that caught the imagination of the whole town.

A player who helped take Stanley to a new dimension was goalkeeper Paul Collings. Stanley lost their two registered 'keepers in two consecutive games at the very start of the 1992/93 season, and Phil Staley had just three days to find a replacement. Collings proved to be an inspired acquisition. He had been an England Schoolboys' international and he quickly displayed his talent with a stunning penalty save in his second game at home to Leek. The Stanley defence clearly grew in confidence with a 'keeper of Collings' quality behind them. He played only 27 games for Stanley, but was on the losing side just three times.

Accrington Stanley v. Bradford Park Avenue, FA Cup second qualifying round, 26 September 1992. Paul Beck outjumps the Park Avenue defence in what was a routine 2-0 victory for Stanley. The third qualifying round provided a much bigger obstacle when Stanley were drawn away at Conference side Stalybridge Celtic. In what was the finest performance of a distinguished season, Stanley outclassed Stalybridge from start to finish, for a thoroughly deserved 2-1 victory. This earned Stanley a home tie against Northern League side Northallerton Town in the fourth and final qualifying round. By this time, the town was abuzz with FA Cup fever, and 1,159 fans saw Stanley defeat Northallerton 3-1 in an absorbing contest.

Stanley drew Conference side Gateshead at home in the FA Cup first round, and it turned into a memorable occasion in front of a sell-out 2,270 crowd. *Above:* A seventh minute goal from Paul Beck was an ideal start for Stanley. There was a minor scare when the surge of the crowd buckled the railing behind the goal, though fortunately no one was hurt. Gateshead equalised two minutes later and looked the better side for prolonged periods of the first half. *Below:* Just six minutes into the second half, Beck meets a Paul Burns cross and places a first time volley past the Gateshead 'keeper to put Stanley 2-1 up. Beck scored an almost identical third, and despite a second Gateshead goal, Stanley held on for a famous 3-2 victory.

Stanley's reward for their defeat of Gateshead was a second round tie at home to Crewe Alexandra. Not surprisingly, the profile of the club was rising, and here Paul Beck obliges the media with a photo call at the Crown Ground. Highlights of the first round tie against Gateshead had been the subject of a well-wrought short film on *Match of the Day*, the first time the cameras of the famous BBC programme had visited Accrington Stanley. The draw against Crewe posed many logistical problems. With Stanley only able to offer away fans a minimal number of tickets, the decision was taken to transfer the game to Ewood Park. This allowed Stanley to maximise the income from the tie, but there was also some regret that Stanley's biggest home game for over thirty years had to be relocated outside the town.

Above: Action from Accrington Stanley *v.* Crewe, Ewood Park, 5 December 1992. Paul Beck is tripped just short of the Crewe penalty area. The chasing Crewe defender on the far right is ex-Stanley man Gus Wilson. *Below:* A young Stanley fan reflects sadly on a 1-6 defeat, a disappointing outcome, but the scoreline merely emphasised the superb finishing of Crewe, who took every chance they created. The crowd of 10,801 was the highest FA Cup attendance of the day, and they gave Stanley a deserved ovation from the field. Just a few weeks later, Crewe paid Stanley a fee of £10,000 for full-back Martin Clark.

A trio of influential Stanley regulars. *Above left:* Mike Lutkevitch was one of the most respected non-League strikers of his day who had scored an FA Trophy final goal at Wembley. He contributed with two vital goals and much inspired forward wing play in the 1992/93 FA Cup run. *Above right:* Phil Collins has the honour of meeting Ashley Hoskin, an immensely skilful winger who enjoyed an excellent rapport with the Stanley fans. *Left:* Left-back Steve Lampkin was an automatic choice for the duration of his stay at Stanley, and with Martin Clark briefly formed a wing-back partnership of the highest quality.

117

Above: New Accrington Stanley boss Ken Wright (second left) at Turf Moor, Sunday 14 November 1993. A disagreement with the board, itself partly due to a poor run of form, resulted in Phil Staley's departure from the Crown Ground just days before a crucial FA Cup fourth qualifying round tie at Conference side Altrincham. The Board moved quickly to appoint Ken Wright as Staley's replacement. Like Staley, Wright was a vastly experienced non-League manager, but he had precious little time to prepare the team for the Altrincham showdown. Against most expectations, however, Stanley absorbed over an hour of Altrincham pressure, before two brilliant breakaway goals from Paul Beck secured a memorable 2-0 victory. Stanley's reward was a first round home tie against Scunthorpe United. Once again, Stanley took the decision to switch the game, this time locking horns with League opposition at Turf Moor.

Opposite, top: Action from the FA Cup first round tie against Scunthorpe United. Jim Connor (far right) turns in celebration after scoring Stanley's second equaliser in the eighty-ninth minute. The other Stanley players are Paul Beck (10) and Chris Wood (2).

Bottom: Charlie Cooper walks dejectedly from the Turf Moor pitch. With just seconds remaining and every Accrington fan dreaming of a midweek replay, Stanley failed to clear a corner and Scunthorpe snatched a sickening last-kick-of-the-game winner to go through 3-2. Ken Wright's reign as manager lasted just four months as he struggled to alleviate Stanley's relegation worries. Eric Whalley returned for his second spell as Stanley manager, and he inspired the club to a confident finish that saw them comfortably avoid relegation and reach two cup semi-finals.

Three Stanley players, from left: Paul Beck, Ashley Hoskin and John Hughes, with the Accrington Stanley Norwegian Supporters Club, November 1993. The Norwegian appetite for English football is well known, and in January 1993 an enthusiastic group of Norwegians adopted Stanley and formed a Norwegian Supporters' Club. In the course of two visits to Accrington, the Scandinavians generated a considerable amount of publicity for Stanley. In the same year, they competed in the British Clubs' Supporters' Cup, an annual Norwegian event. They created quite a stir – not only because they were the only team representing a non-League club – but also due to the fact that they defeated supporters' teams representing Ipswich, West Ham, Wolves, Leeds United and Liverpool to take the trophy.

In February 1994, striker Phil Hutchinson had the honour of receiving the *Mail on Sunday* Player of the Month award for the Northern Premier League. Hutchinson burst onto the non-League scene at Stanley in the second half of the 1993/94 season and for a time looked to have established a productive partnership with Paul Beck. However, this period saw a slow decline in Stanley's fortunes and Hutchinson struggled to maintain his form during the following season.

March 1995 saw another big occasion for Stanley fans when Blackburn Rovers provided the opposition in the Stanley Centenary game. Rovers were in their Premiership pomp, with a host of star players, and Stanley found themselves facing the likes of Tim Sherwood, Kevin Gallacher and Chris Sutton at a redeveloped Ewood Park that bore little resemblance to the stadium in which they had entertained Crewe in 1992. Les Thompson, a recent recruit from Burnley, was Stanley skipper.

Stanley 'keeper Rob Mulloy in action during the Centenary game. The two Rovers players nearest to the camera are Kevin Gallacher (*left*) and Mike Newell (*right*). Mulloy and Stanley's other 'keeper Rob Holcroft, each playing a half, had inspirational games and Stanley acquitted themselves well in front of 8,000 spectators. The game finished in a 2-0 victory for the hosts. The Stanley players who took part that night were: Mulloy, Grimshaw, Thompson, Quick, Sanders, Clarkson, Rushby, Rogerson, McNally, Welch, Robinson, Hoskin, Holcroft, Beck, Bursnell and Raywood.

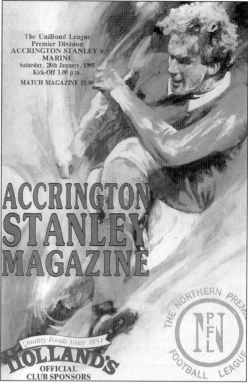

Above left: Chris Grimshaw with friends in Barbados, July 1995. In the close season of 1995, Stanley were invited to Barbados to compete in a tournament with representative and club sides from Barbados. Stanley excelled themselves, winning both games and with it the Anglo-Barbados Cup. *Above right:* The programme for Accrington Stanley's fixture *v.* Marine, 28 January 1995. This game was significant in that it was the first under the new chairmanship of Eric Whalley. Whalley's purchase of a controlling stake in the club heralded the end of John Alty's long reign as chairman. Alty had taken over as chairman in 1981, and his period in office had seen Stanley go from a small Cheshire League club to one of the biggest concerns in the Northern Premier League. Alty succeeded in raising the profile of the club, using its famous name to generate sponsorship deals and merchandising contracts, increasing the club's income in the process. Some may have thought it wrong to let the Milk Marketing Board ridicule Accrington Stanley, but the bottom line for the chairman was that it brought in thousands of pounds and lots of media interest.

Alty's chairmanship was grounded in a desire to see the club return to the Football League, and part of his strategy was always to maintain a rate of visible progress, be it through ground developments or results on the pitch. The problem was what to do when Stanley hit a glass ceiling, as clubs on the rise invariably do. On a couple of occasions, Alty appealed to the public with a warning of impending doom if support didn't improve. On other occasions, there were well-publicised all-out drives for promotion. Rarely did any of these measures drastically improve matters. In any case, Stanley were already a relatively well-supported club, and not everyone shared the chairman's desire to get back in the Football League at all costs. By the time of Alty's departure, the era of Staley and the FA Cup adventures were a fading memory, and ground improvements had also ceased. It was no doubt a disappointment for Alty to leave Stanley with the club struggling in the Northern Premier League and stuck in something of a rut. But on the whole his chairmanship was one of modest and piecemeal success, even if he would have liked to have achieved much more.

Accrington Stanley, 1996/97. From left to right, back row: Ian Rishton (coach), Ged Walsh, Lee Rogerson, Rob Mulloy, Daryl Sloan, Darren Quick, Andy Burns, Tony Briffa, Phil Leather (kit man), Jimmy Coffey (assistant manager). Middle row: John McNally, Brent Peters (director), Iain McClellan, Stan Allen (manager), Peter Mellor, Chris Mulloy. Front: Neil Edmunds, Brett Ormerod, Mark Rawstron, Ollie Parillon, Darren Thornton, Brian Welch.

Tony Greenwood replaced Stan Allen as manager of Accrington Stanley in August 1996. The previous year, Greenwood had guided Preston side Bamber Bridge to the championship of the Northern Premier League (by this time the Unibond League), despite having only limited resources at his disposal. It was hoped that he could do the same for Stanley, but he was given little time to prove himself and was sacked in September 1997. In March of the same year, Blackpool bought Brett Ormerod for £50,000, then the largest fee by far that Stanley had received for a player.

The signing of Paul Moulden (*left*), a striker who had been a teenage prodigy with Manchester City, heightened hopes for the 1997/98 season. Although Moulden had failed to fulfil his potential in the Football League, he was still considered to be a good player who was expected to do well for Stanley. A bright start saw Liverpool Reserves soundly defeated 3-0 in a pre-season friendly, but both Moulden and the team in general failed to make an impact on the Unibond League title race. Once more, Stanley fans had to put up with a season of dour league struggle.

Non-League is not a place for faint hearts, and that applies also to referees. Stanley's Greg Challender lets the referee know what he thinks in this 1998 League encounter at the Crown Ground.

Accrington Stanley line up before the opening pre-season friendly of the 1999/2000 season against Wrexham, July 1999. From left to right, back row: Paul Tomlinson, Billy O'Callaghan, Paul Heavey, Mark Howard, Jamie Speare, Neil Thornton, Ged Walsh, Aidan Warder, John Coleman (player-manager). Front row: Robbie Williams, Mark Brennan, Jimmy Bell (assistant manager), Steve Carragher, Mark Shirley, Jay Flannery, James Gedman, Eamon Elliot. The 1998/99 campaign had finally seen happen what many Stanley fans had thought was in the air for the previous few seasons – relegation to the Unibond First Division. The only consolation of the 1998/99 campaign was the form of Billy O'Callaghan, who scored 32 goals to win the divisional golden boot award, quite an achievement in a relegation-bound side. Stanley took the opportunity to undergo a wholesale clearout of personnel and appointed a new managerial team in the form of John Coleman and Jimmy Bell, a duo with experience in the Unibond First Division. They brought in many new faces and though early season form was initially shaky, the team soon hit their stride and began to make an impression on the First Division promotion race.

Also apparent from this photograph are the ground improvements instigated under the chairmanship of Eric Whalley. Visible behind the team is the additional seating along the side and under the executive boxes which increased the number of seats at the Crown Ground to 600. Also visible is the cantilever roof structure that brought all the seating under one cover. In 2001, this roof was extended to completely cover the length of the pitch. In addition, terracing was built behind each goal to accommodate a total of 4,000 spectators. By the beginning of the 2001/02 season, Accrington Stanley will have a ground that conforms to required Football Conference and Football League standards.

The acquisition of Gary Williams from Ashton Town in August 1999 was a key signing. Williams made what must rate as one of the quickest scoring debuts on record, netting after just 14 seconds on his first appearance at Burscough. His pace and finishing prowess proceeded to cause havoc in opposition defences. In January 2000, 34 appearances and 24 goals later, Williams was sold to Conference side Doncaster Rovers for £60,000, the most lucrative transfer yet for Stanley. The impetus that Williams' goals gave to the team helped to set Stanley on their way to an exciting final half of the season.

Another important signing was that of centre half Jonathan Smith, who arrived at Stanley from neighbours Great Harwood Town. An imposing presence at the heart of the defence, Smith also proved invaluable at set-pieces, from which he scored most of his 8 goals during the 1999/2000 season. Fewer were more important than the equaliser in a must-win game at promotion rivals Ratcliffe Borough on Easter Monday. Amidst wild scenes of celebration from 800 travelling fans, Stanley came from 0-2 down to win 3-2 and set themselves up for two final home games, from which they needed maximum points to win promotion.

Stanley player-manager John Coleman celebrates Stanley's second goal in the 3-0 victory over Farsley Celtic that secured the Unibond First Division title in front of 2,468 at the Crown Ground, on 6 May 2000. It was a triumph for the new managerial team, who were not immune to criticism, particularly about alleged tactics of exerting authority upon games by fair means or foul before going for goals. In reality, Coleman and Bell succeeded in re-establishing some much-needed steel into the Stanley game that complemented the considerable skills of ball players like Mark Shirley, Russell Payne and Jay Flannery. In winning the Unibond First Division, Stanley became the first team to regain their Premier League status at the first time of asking, and also set the club up once more for a tilt at the Football Conference.

Stanley started the 2000/01 season as they had left off the previous campaign, but a sustained challenge proved a step too far. However, Stanley's final placing of ninth was their highest since the days of Phil Staley. The acquisition of Liam Watson for £15,000 and Gary Williams for a club record £25,000 demonstrated that ambition burns brightly at the club and that ground improvements do not spell the end of team building. Accrington Stanley are certainly a more financially robust outfit than ever before. The support attracted to the Crown Ground during the final days of the 1999/2000 season was also grist to the mill of those who remain convinced that a place in the Football League should be Accrington Stanley's rightful target. There is little doubt that the foundations being laid today by Eric Whalley and the backroom staff at the Crown Ground could see this dream come to fruition.

Peel Park today. Little evidence exists of a Football League club or its 26,000 capacity stadium. The Peel Park Hotel still guards the ground, and the small block of changing rooms opposite contains the stone plaque that reminds observers that the modest construction was the effort of the Supporters' Club of 1937.

A great virtue of British football is the continuity it brings to the local histories of multitudes of towns and cities throughout the country. Governments change, new industries prosper and then decline, communities are shifted between different municipal boundaries. One thing that tends to remain is the football club, an organic, living thing that embodies the collective identity of a community. But identity requires comprehension to make it real. To be an Accringtonian – to have that as part of your identity – is not just to live within or to come from the locality, but to know and understand something about the place itself.

For millions of people, it is their football club that makes their identity real. This is why a football club is important to a locality. With a football club, a town provides so much more scope for its people to forge a sense of belonging and, even more importantly, to generate some civic pride and loyalty. It will forever be a great shame that Accrington lost its original version of Stanley in 1962, and that school playing field to the north of the town centre will always echo with the ghostly cries of a club that was allowed to die. But today's Stanley was founded by people who were there in 1962, and the hope behind all their endeavour was that those past mistakes could be, if not forgiven, at least understood and never allowed to happen again. It was those people who, quietly, would admit that their ultimate dream was to see Stanley back in the Football League, even when the system offered no hope of automatic promotion. The road to the prize of the Football League is long – perhaps the longest and most arduous in British football – but it might yet take Accrington Stanley back to their Football League home. Which is why today's Stanley deserves the support of its townspeople. It isn't the club that competed in the Football League, but it continues the same traditions and embodies the same hopes. In the world of football, that ought to be enough.